For Connie, Dan, Edward, Hannah and Jake

Frances Lincoln Ltd
4 Torriano Mews
Torriano Avenue
London NW5 2RZ
www.franceslincoln.com
www.goingwild.net

Run Wild!
Copyright © Frances Lincoln 2011
Text copyright © Fiona Danks and Jo Schofield 2011
Photographs copyright © Jo Schofield and Fiona Danks 2011

Designed by Sarah Slack

First Frances Lincoln edition: 2011

A catalogue record for this book is available from the British Library.

ISBN 9780711231726

Printed and bound in China

9 8 7 6 5 4 3 2 1

This book contains some potentially dangerous activities. Please note that any reader, or anyone in their charge, taking part in any of the activities described does so at their own risk. Neither the author nor the publisher can accept any legal responsibility for any harm, injury, damage, loss or prosecution resulting from the use or misuse of the activities, techniques, tools and advice in the book.

 It is illegal to carry out any of these activities on private land without the owner's permission. Please obey all laws relating to the protection of land, property, plants and animals.

RUN WILD!

OUTDOOR GAMES AND ADVENTURES

Fiona Danks and Jo Schofield

CONTENTS

RUN WILD!

The excited chattering of the class of four- and five-year-olds was almost drowned out by the drumming of the rain on the school roof that chilly February afternoon. 'Oh, we go out for Forest School every Tuesday afternoon, come rain or shine,' said their enthusiastic teacher while helping the children to wrap up in warm clothes, waterproofs and wellies.

As we walked to the nearby wood the whole class chanted, 'We're all going on a puddle hunt', though the adult helpers looked decidedly unconvinced. The children jumped and splashed in every single puddle, and when someone broke a layer of ice they all looked through ice windows and made ice monsters in the mud. As we walked further the rain eased, so we collected seeds and twigs to make simple percussion instruments to accompany a rain dance, because everyone wanted even more puddles. Later the children huddled in their den (made on a previous visit), eating soggy biscuits and drinking hot chocolate cooled by raindrops. Before long they were off again, puddle jumping all the way back to school. Amazingly nobody seemed to notice the cold, be bothered by the mud or worry about getting wet; wrapped cosily in winter waterproofs, they had all enjoyed another adventure in the woods.

Run Wild! aims to inspire parents, teachers, scout and guide leaders and anyone working or playing with groups of children to have fun outdoors – anywhere, anytime, whatever the age of the children, whatever the weather. If you are organizing a children's party or a gathering of friends or family, a school field trip or an outing for a youth organization, there are activity ideas and practical projects suitable for all sorts of occasions, from outdoor games and following trails to woodland storytelling and planting trees. *Run Wild!* provides opportunities for real excitement, real emotions, open-ended imaginary play and surviving dirty clothes and grazed knees.

Taking a large group out can be daunting, but *Run Wild!* is packed with suggestions to make it easier, providing ideas suitable for adapting for different groups of children in a wide range of outdoor environments. The activities might take a little planning and organization, and should always be carried out with respect for the natural world, but they won't cost much and they will be fun for everybody. Outdoors is the perfect place for celebrating birthdays, anniversaries, achievements, special occasions or the moment; there is a separate chapter on parties, but many of the other activities described in the book would add to a celebration.

The natural world offers endless opportunities for exciting, exhilarating experiences. Go out in a hoar frost when every twig and blade of grass is covered in icy thorns; get up early and surround yourself with a woodland dawn chorus; get soaked in a sudden downpour; or climb to the summit of a hill on a blustery day

to feel the wind try to lift you off the ground. Moments like these stay sharply etched in the memory, effecting a long-lasting connection with nature. Bristling with opportunities for exercising muscles, stretching imaginations, challenging minds, releasing creativity and learning new skills, the wild world offers joy and freedom. An increasing body of research indicates that being active in the green outdoors improves physical and mental health and fosters stronger social bonds. We have often witnessed for ourselves how being together in wild places brings family and group members together, encouraging communication and openness.

But it can, we know, be difficult to get children outside. Being indoors is safe, easy and comfortable. You can have the whole world at your fingertips through the Internet and social networking sites, plus the fun of endless electronic games. Influenced by such distractions, as well as commercial and peer pressure – the pressure to be cool, to wear the right clothes, to do and buy the right things – children often resist. So how can we tempt today's PlayStation generation to go outdoors? Time and again we have enticed our children into the natural world by inviting some friends along and having plenty of fun ideas up our sleeves. And how about using IT to tempt them? Try taking digital photos of an activity to upload on to a school website or social networking page or email to friends; use global positioning devices and mobile phones for treasure hunts. Recording an outdoor play on a camcorder, video camera or even a mobile phone is another way in which children's interest in such things can be combined with having fun outdoors.

On a rare snowy day our teenage sons dashed outside to make the most of the weather. Dressed in their designer trainers and logo-branded hoodies, they disappeared up the hill with some friends and a couple of old plastic sacks. The snow had been sledged to oblivion but they still hurled themselves off the top of the hill, rocketing bodies parting from plastic sacks as they slid down a mudslide, shrieking with laughter. As soon as they reached the bottom they dashed back up for another go, their carefully chosen outfits now plastered in mud. The washing machine coped, the clothes recovered and we still smile at the memory of those big boys losing their inhibitions and experiencing the freedom of running wild.

From this and countless other experiences with our families and friends we know that once children go outside and get stuck in, with little more than their imagination, resourcefulness and a sense of fun they can have endless good times, some of which we have described here. But Run Wild! is about more than good times: it's also about reconnecting children with the wonders of biodiversity and discovering how to enjoy wild places with minimum impact and maximum respect. How can we expect future generations to value our countryside and the pockets of wildness in our cities if they don't get out there and experience it for real? We hope that this book will help adults give more children opportunities to get out into nature and touch it, smell it, hear it and see it with their very own eyes and find their wild side. So don't wait for that perfect day – just dress for the weather, grab your wellies, coat or sunhat and Run Wild!

WILD THEATRE

COSTUMES

MASKS

BODY AND FACE PAINTING

PUPPETS AND MAGICAL CREATURES

MUSICAL INSTRUMENTS

WILD THEATRE

The natural world – whether in a woodland glade, on a wild sweeping hillside, among twisted trees in the park or at the bottom of the garden – is a perfect place for pretending, providing a special atmosphere even the most talented set designers couldn't conjure up.

Anya and Frankie performed an outdoor play about a wicked greedy lion who left the dry, empty plains to go and live in a forest full of tasty creatures, but the magical fairies of the forest ran rings around the conceited lion and chased him back to the plains. Their make-up was berries and chalk; the fairy was dressed in leaves and ferns. Everyone had great fun decorating the stage with woven ivy, vines, rosehips and brightly coloured leaves. Fairy lights provided the finishing touch to this natural play in a natural setting, but we could have added night lights in jars or made our own tissue and twig lanterns to add to the magical atmosphere.

During one of our parties, children and young teenagers performed plays on an improvised garden stage. The very fact that they were outdoors seemed to inspire and excite them; they had a completely free rein and came up with a hilarious hotchpotch of stories with bizarre characters dressed in intriguing and imaginative home-made costumes. Each five-minute play was filmed on a camcorder and when the parents arrived everyone watched the performances on TV, which added to the excitement.

Wild theatre – plays in outdoor settings using props, puppets and costumes designed from nature – can be a wonderful way to let imaginations fly, as well as bringing people together and helping them develop a deeper relationship with the natural world. This chapter provides a few ideas for using wild places and natural materials to release creativity and make theatre come alive.

COSTUMES

Deep in the woods you might find the king and queen of the forest, dressed in richly decorated cloaks and crowns and disguised with masks. Or you might find Gandalf from *Lord of the Rings*, mythical creatures, wild animals and birds or the Green Man himself, a magical character who blends in with the trees. Distinguishing these characters are their wonderful costumes, made from feathers, leaves and other natural materials. Try making your own wild costumes: start by taking the fancy-dress box outside and then use a few simple natural materials, some natural face paints (see page 87) and whatever else nature has to offer.

HEADDRESSES AND CROWNS

Many traditional cultures used natural head-dresses to draw attention to the head, where they believed the soul or spirit resided. The wearing of a crown also implies high rank and importance. This colourful creation made of exotic autumn leaves and feathery ferns is quite as beautiful a crown as a jewel-encrusted one. Have a go at making crowns and head-dresses using natural and recycled materials.

What you need

- Strips of card (e.g. from cereal packets)
- Double-sided sticky tape and thin wire
- Natural materials such as feathers, leaves, seeds and grasses

Making a headdress or crown

Make a base and then add whatever decorations you wish.

- **Willow base** Twist thin bendy willow around to make a circle. Thread leaves through it and attach seeds with thin wires.
- **Card base** Cover a length of card with double-sided tape. Stick on leaves and seeds to make a crown, or feathers to make a headdress.
- **Evergreen branch** Coil a length of branch to make a circle and fix it with wire. Decorate it with seeds and cones attached with fine wires.
- **Cleavers** This scrambling annual plant, also known as goosegrass or sticky-willy, covered in tiny hooked bristles, sticks to itself and everything else. Anya twisted a bunch of it into a crown and decorated it with flowers gathered during a walk – one of each type she found.

WILD CLOAKS

At Hannah's fourteenth birthday party, three teams competed to dress a girl for a ball, using just a pile of old newspapers and a bit of tape. After about twenty minutes and much giggling, each team had produced the most amazing outfit, complete with hat and shoes.

We have played a similar game at family parties using old wrapping paper and a couple of bin bags to dress someone as a favourite film character. Try playing a version of this dressing-up game out in the woods: can you create a costume using only sticks, grasses, leaves and perhaps a little netting and wool? We got the idea for this spectacular outfit after seeing traditional Maori cloaks made from flax and feathers.

MAKING A WILD CLOAK

● Start with some soft fabric with a fine mesh, such as old net curtains or garden netting. We used 1m/1yd of shelter shade mesh purchased from a garden centre.
● Thread brightly coloured leaves through the mesh. We made a random pattern, but covering the whole cloak with leaves would be even more impressive.
● If the leaves won't fix securely (if the holes are too large the leaves will fall out), use wool, double-sided tape, elastic bands or twist ties to attach them.
● Use the cloak immediately before the leaves fade and wilt.

COSTUME JEWELLERY

Costume jewellery is larger than life, adding drama and glamour to a costume. Common flowers such as the daisy and dandelion make wonderful garlands, necklaces, bracelets and headbands. Or find colourful leaves from the woods or fallen petals from a garden. Threaded on to wool, they will make a dramatic necklace or perhaps a chain of office.

MASKS

Masks transform the wearer into someone else; they can be strangely liberating and unnervingly powerful. Make some wild masks to conjure up fun, mystery, magic or menace. If children are uncomfortable about covering their faces, they might prefer to use a Venetian-style mask or a hat mask.

LEAFY MASKS

What you need

- Cardboard mask template or a cheap plastic mask
- Card from an old cereal box or plastic from an old milk container
- Double-sided sticky tape, scissors, Plasticine, PVA glue or wallpaper paste, aluminium foil, cling film
- Modroc (plaster of Paris bandage, available from good art and craft suppliers)
- A straight stick about 30cm/12in long
- A selection of autumn leaves – use them fresh or press them for a couple of weeks in a telephone directory to make them flat and supple
- Other materials for decoration, e.g. feathers, charcoal, chalk, seeds, dried grasses, bark

Making a half-mask

Inspired by a trip to Venice, Connie and Helena made elegant half-masks.

- Draw around the template on the plastic or card, and then cut out the mask shape.
- Stick double-sided tape over the mask and cut out eyeholes.
- Stick leaves, grasses and/or feathers firmly all over the mask.
- Attach more leaves around the edge to decorate. Add other details as you wish – perhaps feathers, petals or ferns – or paint white patterns with a natural chalk paint (see page 89).
- Paint the mask with diluted PVA glue for a better finish.
- Cover the stick in double-sided tape and then wrap leaves tightly around it. Tape the stick to one side of the mask (the right-hand side if you are right-handed).

Making a full mask

We made this full mask by sticking autumn leaves over a cheap plastic mask, but you could cut out a mask shape in card or plastic.

● Use Plasticine to build up the features, perhaps a hooked nose, animal ears and fierce teeth – make whatever gruesome or beautiful disguise you wish.

● To add a crown or headdress, stick appropriate cardboard shapes to the top of the mask.

● Cover the whole thing in aluminium foil and use this as your mask; or, if you have more time, cover it in cling film and use it as a template to make masks out of Modroc. Cut the Modroc into short lengths and soak them in water before placing several overlapping layers over the template. Remove the template when the Modroc has dried into shape.

● Cover your mask in leaves, sticking them on firmly with double-sided tape, diluted PVA glue or wallpaper paste. Where the mask is curved, use smaller pieces of leaf; otherwise they won't stick very well.

● Decorate with feathers or larger leaves if you wish.

OTHER MASK IDEAS

● Be inspired by mythology: make a mask for the oak king, who rules from mid-winter to mid-summer, or for the more sinister holly king, who rules from mid-winter to mid-summer.

● Create a full Green Man effect by covering and surrounding the mask with green leaves and then adding ivy, vines or other creepers to sprout from the nose, mouth and eyes.

● Make a shaman mask by hanging feathers from the sides and adding antlers or horns made from twigs.

ANIMAL HAT MASKS

Simple animal masks on hat frames transform children into wild creatures for an outdoor play or a game.

Making a hat mask

● Cut two lengths of cardboard, each about 5cm/2in wide by 30cm/12in long. Fix them together in a cross.

● Cut another length of card about 5cm/2in wide by 60cm/24in long. Bend this piece round to make a circle to fit your head; fix the ends together with tape.

● Curve the cross of card over the circle and attach it as shown to make a frame to fit on your head.

● Cut out a head shape of an animal and then fit it on the front of the frame; the mask can either hang down over the face or be more of a hat. Paint the animal mask (perhaps using natural paints) and decorate with natural materials to make berry eyes, leafy ears, twig antlers or stick horns.

BODY AND FACE PAINTING

Evidence from prehistoric tomb paintings and sculptures, as well as from more recent non-Western cultures, shows the enduring popularity of face and body painting, as do the long queues whenever face painting or henna decorating is on offer at a community event or a school fair. Originally the painted markings and patterns were believed to have magical powers that warded off evil spirits or enemies, but they were also used to signify social status and celebrate special occasions and events.

An Australian friend showed us pictures of aboriginal body painting, explaining how the designs related to the spirituality of ancestors, animals and the land. Inspired by these tales we set off for the woods, where the children pounded chalk to make white paint to daub over faces, hands, arms and bodies. But aboriginal designs used a varied palette of brown, orange and ochre, so we experimented, using earth to make brown and mixing clay with chalk to make orange. Everyone, whether three or fifteen years old, had a wonderful time, returning home happy and calm, and covered in weird patterns. The idea of dreamtime and ancient aboriginal stories had captured the girls' imagination. They searched for animals in the woods, depicting them in drawings on their arms and hands, bark and stones. They spent the rest of the afternoon at the computer, writing a vivid story about snails and witches. For once we had no objection to their screen-based activities.

What you need

- Non-toxic natural pigments, such as clay, charcoal or burnt cork, chalk and wild berries including elder and blackberry
- A pestle and mortar
- Paintbrushes, small sponges and water
- Beaten egg white or unscented cold cream to mix with the pigment

Making and using the paints

- Sieve or grind the natural pigments to make as fine a paste or powder as possible; gritty face paint is ineffective and uncomfortable. Chalk must be pounded with a heavy stone or metal pestle to make a smooth powder.
- Mix each pigment with water, egg white or cold cream to make a smooth, creamy paint.
- Check for allergy by painting on a small area of skin before painting patterns on the face or body with brushes, sponges or fingers.
- Experiment with patterns and pictures. How about a chalk skeleton for Hallowe'en or a lizard inspired by aboriginal body painting?

Safety tips

- **Only use egg white if no one is allergic to eggs. If using cold cream, use a hypo-allergenic brand.**
- **Collect non-toxic berries and other materials from clean, unpolluted sites.**
- **Avoid getting paint near anyone's eyes.**

PUPPETS AND MAGICAL CREATURES

Oxford's Pitt Rivers Museum contains two ancient wooden figures decorated with moss, each one about 15cm/6in high. They came from a remote part of Russia where people once worshipped a god who guarded the forests; perhaps the figures were used to pass on beliefs. Dolls and puppets have been carved from wood and modelled in clay across many cultures, used to pass on traditions and stories as well as used in children's play. Making imaginary creatures and characters like these can be a fun way to create magical drama with limited resources, bringing the inanimate to life.

Try looking at natural materials in new and imaginative ways. Could berries or tiny pebbles become eyes? Could a seed become a nose, ash keys become feathers or lichen-covered twigs become bird's feet or a deer's antlers? Here are a few suggestions for creating your own menagerie of creatures and mystical characters.

Perhaps you could also invent magical worlds for them to live in, work out what they might eat and who might eat them, and take them off for all sorts of wonderful adventures. If you have a camcorder, a video camera or even a mobile phone, have a go at making an animated film about them.

MARIONETTE PUPPETS

We saw the most wonderful marionette birds made from plastic bags during a workshop run by Gordon MacLellan, aka Creeping Toad, and decided to try making similar puppets using natural and recycled materials. This basic method of making a bird puppet can be adapted to make anything from dragons and monsters to creepy crawlies and other wild creatures.

What you need

- Scrap fabric and card
- Sticks, twigs
- String and newspaper
- Glue (a hot glue gun works best)
- Masking tape, double-sided tape
- Elastic bands
- Natural materials – leaves, seeds, feathers, etc.

Making the puppet

- Cut out a fabric square about 65cm/26in by 65cm/26in; the size will depend on what you are making.
- Roll some newspaper into a tight ball. Place it in the centre of the square, roll the fabric round it and put an elastic band in place as shown to make the head.
- To make a long floppy neck, put a second elastic band about 5cm/2in from the first elastic band.
- Make a larger newspaper ball for a body. Place it in the fabric next to the neck and fix it in place with another elastic band. The end of loose fabric will become the tail.
- Cut out some cardboard wings and attach to the body with doubled-sided tape or tuck them under the elastic band. Alternatively find some large leaves or feathers to make wings, as in the dragon bird illustrated here.

- Decorate your puppet with natural materials. Cover the wings, the body and tail and make eyes and a beak. This dragon bird has a teasel head with acorn cup and berry eyes. Some materials could be poked through the elastic bands to secure them in place, but elsewhere use a hot glue gun, PVA glue or tape.

- To make a jointed leg, place two twigs end to end with 1cm/½ in gap between them on a piece of masking tape. Roll the tape around the sticks and the gap in between them to make a leg with a flexible joint. Alternatively, place the twigs end to end and tape a length of string along their lengths so that they can bend in the middle.

- Finally, find two straight sticks and tape or tie them together in an X shape. Tie a string on to the end of each stick and attach the other end of the strings to the wings, the head and the tail to make your very own characterful marionette.

- You could make smaller puppets from old socks. Add twig legs and berry eyes to make anything from a spider to a pig.

A FRUIT CATERPILLAR

What creatures can you make by threading fruits or seeds along a string? We made this caterpillar with medlars, knotting the string between each fruit; the spiky tops of each medlar made perfect caterpillar feet. We attached cotton to each end so that it could even be made to move like a caterpillar.

HOUSES, CASTLES AND KINGDOMS

Perhaps the imaginary creatures you have made need a place to live in or a kingdom in which to reign. Encourage children to make little houses or elaborate castles from loose natural materials. This house made of twigs covered in grass and moss was made for a shy troll, who installed a big antenna (a tall twig) to keep the scary birds away.

WIGGLY STICK SNAKE

I remember being fascinated by a toy snake with a jointed body. When held by the tail it seemed to slither and squirm just like a real snake. When fiddling with an elder twig one day I wondered if I could make a natural version, a wiggly stick snake.

What you need
- An elder stick
- A length of fabric or ribbon about 1.5cm/½ in wide and about 30cm/12in long
- Secateurs and glue
(we used a hot glue gun)
- Natural paints

Making the snake
- Using secateurs, cut the elder stick into 2.5cm/1in lengths. Carefully split each piece in half lengthways.
- Glue one half of each length on to one side of the ribbon and the other half on the other side, so that there are matching pairs along its length.
- Use a thicker piece of elder as the snake's head, and make a leaf tongue.
- Paint with chalk and other natural paints.

Safety tip

- **Supervise children at all times when using secateurs and hot glue.**

HAND AND FOOT PUPPETS

Can you transform your hands into birds, snails, butterflies or other funny characters with natural paints? Draw some eyes on little pieces of card and stick these on hands and feet. Can you make more elaborate puppets using several pairs of hands or feet?

A great game is to use your whole body to make puppets with your friends. Perhaps three people could become a tree, four people a spider, or a large group a millipede. This is a wonderful way to bring theatre into learning (How many legs or body parts do they have? Can they make a story about their characters? If they are an oak, is the tree happy or grumpy?).

HOBBY ANIMALS

I remember galloping off down the garden for all sorts of imaginary adventures on my hobby-horse. But how about making other hobby animals – perhaps deer, foxes, bears or even a unicorn or a dragon – to play with outdoors? I always seem to have a collection of odd socks (where do all the other socks go?), the perfect starting point for hobby animals. The secret to success is in getting the details right: it is the ears, eyes, antlers or horns that bring them to life.

What you need
- Socks, newspaper, double-sided tape and string, pipe cleaners or twist ties
- A long stick for the pole and smaller twigs for antlers or a unicorn's horn
- Leaves and seeds to make ears and eyes

Making a hobby animal
- Stuff a sock with scrunched-up newspaper. Choose what animal you are making (this might depend on the colour of the sock) and shape the stuffed sock accordingly. Push a stick right in to the sock and then fix the open end of the sock to the stick with a twist tie, pipe cleaner or tape.
- Using double-sided tape, stick on seed eyes, leafy ears and a twig mouth to bring your animal to life. We poked two forked twigs into the top of the sock to make antlers for our stag.
- How will your animal behave? Perhaps everyone has made a different animal; if so, how will they interact? Have fun galloping off under the trees or across a windy hillside.

CLAY AND TWIG CREATURES

Have you ever found a gnarled and twisted twig that resembled a little person or a funny monster? We have combined such twigs with clay to make all sorts of characters and creatures. Some have become puppets to take part in a show, while others have become the focus of imaginary games. The discovery of a dragon-like curved twig inspired this miniature monster. When we found a forked twig with torn fibres at one end that reminded us of spiky hair, we added clay features and jointed twig arms, stuck on a leafy outfit with double-sided tape and attached sticks with string, allowing us to move the arms and bring our twig man to life. Look for twisted twigs and use a little imagination to create your own monsters and characters.

Making the creatures

● If using clay, work it to make it pliable; then mould into the required shape to enhance your twig.

● Decorate with natural materials to make whatever creature you want.

● Use natural paints (see page 89) to add the finishing touches.

MUSICAL INSTRUMENTS

Natural music is all around us, in the sound of the sea in a conch shell, the gentle tinkling of icicles, the howling of the wind in the trees, birdsong and animal calls. Anything that makes a sound can become a musical or percussion instrument, whether it's two palm-sized flat pebbles that can be struck together (as in Hawaiian castanets) or a can transformed into a guitar. Try making simple instruments from natural and recycled materials to bring stories and theatre alive.

PERCUSSION INSTRUMENTS

When out in the woods with a group of young children we searched for stones, twigs and dry seeds to shake and rattle. We made simple percussion instruments and then performed a rain dance, singing and dancing together as the rain poured down.

What you need
● A collection of natural noises: search for dry seeds, nuts, stones, shells, unripe berries and anything else the children think might make a sound. You can also use noisy rubbish, such as ring pulls and bottle tops.
● Plastic or glass jars, tins with lids or clear plastic bottles
● Forked sticks
● Fine wire

A MARACA

The traditional maraca is a dried gourd filled with seeds which probably originated in Latin America. Have a go at making different maracas by using a variety of natural noisy materials and containers.
● Place natural noisy materials of one type in a jar or tin, filling it only about half full so they can move around and make a noise.
● If using pebbles, put them in a plastic container rather than a glass one.

BRACELETS AND ANKLET RATTLES

Attach shells, dried seeds and small pebbles on to wool or thread to make bracelets or anklets to add your own percussion to a dance.

A WIND CHIME

● Find an interesting stick or piece of driftwood.
● Collect dry shells, seeds, pebbles or anything that will look nice and make a sound.
● Tie these on to your stick, along with some metallic objects such as can lids.
● Hang your wind chime up outside to move and tinkle in the breeze.

A STICK RATTLE

This is based on the ancient sistrum or frame rattle, an African percussion instrument similar to a tambourine.

● Find a stick, with as many forks as you wish.

● Find some eroded shells or seed cases, or non-natural materials such as buttons, bottle tops, ring pulls or small bells to use as rattles.

● Attach a length of fine wire to the top of one of the forks, and thread some rattles along the wire.

● Twist the wire around the top of the next fork. Then thread more rattles along the wire.

● When you have finished, secure the wire by twisting it over itself.

● Decorate the stick if you wish: you could strip the bark off the wood and paint it with natural paints or make it into a story stick (see page 72).

● Your instrument should make a tinkling tambourine sound. The tone will vary according to what materials you have used and the thickness and tautness of the wire.

A CAN GUITAR

Inspired by a can guitar we saw at the Pitt Rivers Museum in Oxford, we decided to make our own version. The key to a good sound is to keep a high tension in the wire.

What you need
- A tin or aluminium can and a button
- A strong forked stick with straight forks the same length as each other
- A smaller straight bit of twig
- Thin high-tensile wire. This must be pulled very tight to create sufficient tension, so use strong wire that won't snap. The wire should be about twice the length of the forked stick.
- A bradawl

Making the guitar
- The safest can to use is a food can, as the top can be easily removed. Using the bradawl, poke a hole in the centre of the bottom of the can.
- Thread the wire through the button and then twist the short end round the main wire to secure. Push the wire all the way through the hole in the bottom of the can until the button lies flat on the can's base.
- Push the forked stick into the can until it touches the bottom; it must not touch the wire.
- Pull the wire as tight as you can and then twist it around the stick just below the fork, as shown. To add tension and improve the sound, take the short stick and slide it between the wire and the forked stick, pulling it down away from the can with your fingers.
- Pluck the wire and see how many different sounds you can make.

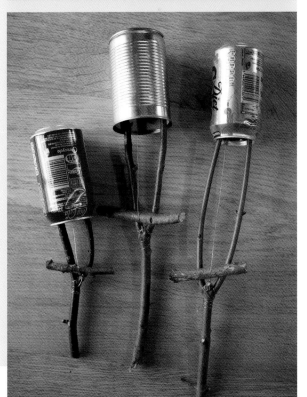

WILD PARTIES

WILD PARTIES

Over the last twenty years or so, we have organized at least eighty-five birthday parties between us. We have braved picnics in the snow, pretended to be aliens discovering the Earth, performed crazy open-air plays and huddled happily beneath tarpaulins, listening to the rain. Regardless of the weather, these outdoor parties were always hugely popular with everyone.

Over recent years the party scene has mushroomed into a multi-million-pound industry, but there are plenty of alternatives to the plastic, pile-it-high party package. Why not stand out from the crowd and organize a thrilling expedition to the woods at night, or some scary stories around a garden campfire? Whether it's a child's birthday party, a family celebration or a gathering of friends, an outdoor party is pretty much guaranteed to offer value for money and a whole host of magical, long-lasting memories.

Outdoor parties needn't be complicated or difficult to organize. Find a suitable location – the local woods, a nearby park or the back garden – and enlist a few parents as helpers (go for the ones who are big kids themselves!). Come up with a theme – pirates, fairies, soldiers, animals, Harry Potter or whatever the current craze might be. Once children are in fancy dress and their imaginations are fired up, they will get into the spirit of the party. We hope this book will provide inspiration for parties for small children and teenagers, for small gardens, urban parks or wild woods, for daytime, night-time and any time of year. Try some of the games from the Wild Games chapter (page 36), or perhaps some outdoor theatre (page 74). Mix and match the ideas here until you discover what works best for you.

If you find the thought of an outdoor party daunting, remember that once children are outdoors and in party mood they are often happy to make their own entertainment. If you're worried about the weather, just ask everyone to dress appropriately, so that they will be ready for anything!

THE INSTANT OUTDOOR PARTY

Every month or so a friend of ours used to send an email inviting several families to bring a plate of food and an outdoor game to a gathering in a local park or at the woods. She always left it to the last minute so that she could check the weather forecast, and it was an easy way for all ages to get together to play games, relax and chat. Someone might organize a game of football or a rounders match, or the children might go off to make a den or hold a mini-Olympics. Everyone shared the load and everyone, from babies to teenagers and adults, had fun. An instant outdoor party like this is a good one to try if the very thought of organizing a party fills you with horror.

WOODLAND PARTIES

My nephew George has had a couple of birthday parties in the woods. Several families meet to hunt for treasure, play hide-and-seek and follow trails. They always finish up at George's favourite spot, where he and his dad have built a den. The children add a few more sticks, play some imaginary games and enjoy a snack before running home for tea.

Parties for young children should be kept simple. A trip down the garden, to the local park or to a small copse can be a huge and exciting adventure in itself for very young children. Let them enjoy the freedom of running in the woods and perhaps looking for treasure. Or try a teddy bears' picnic, an Easter egg hunt or some of the following ideas. If it rains, don't change your plans; just wrap everyone up in waterproofs and wellies, make leaf umbrellas and have a picnic under a tarpaulin shelter.

FAIRY OR ELF PARTY IN A WOODLAND GLADE

How about having a magical fairy feast in the middle of the woods? Find a secluded spot and send someone in advance to hang night lights in jars and tissue lanterns in the trees around a little clearing.

Invite the children to come dressed as fairies or other characters, and then lead them along a trail of arrows made with natural materials or flour, or follow night-light lanterns or fairy gifts hung in trees. Perhaps the children could collect feathers and other natural materials and tie them on to a stick to make a fairy or shaman's wand (see page 73). Have a picnic of fairy cakes in your glade, surrounded by twinkling lights and listening to the woodland sounds.

FLOUR GRENADE AMBUSHES

Our children have been invited to many expensive paintball parties, but why not organize your own version? This version can be done in a garden, using straw bales as cover, but it's much more exciting in the woods, with bases and forts to ambush. To make flour grenades, wrap a spoonful of flour in some kitchen roll, twist the paper round the flour and secure with masking tape.

One of our best ambushes was at night. Boys armed with flour grenades followed a prepared trail of glow sticks through the woods until they came across a stick fort we had made earlier in the day. Suddenly the adults (or in this case big kids!) jumped out from the fort and before long everyone was pelting flour grenades at each other. The rest of the party was spent playing night capture the flag (see page 56) and creeping up torch games.

CATAPULT PAINTBALLING

In another cheat's version of paintballing, we took a crowd of boys to the woods and asked them each to find a Y-shaped stick. After a session on knife safety (see the tool safety tips on page 156), everyone whittled his or her own catapult. We split the boys into two teams and they played a version of capture the flag (see page 40) in which the aim was to take opponents out of the game by firing them with blackberries or flour bombs.

CAMOUFLAGE GAMES

How about inviting everyone to come along in natural-coloured clothes so that they can disappear in the woods? Encourage the children to paint mud on their faces and hands and make camouflage blankets (see page 140). Split them into two teams and send one team off to hide, not by hiding behind anything but by relying on camouflage and behaviour to blend in to the background. After a few minutes, send the other team off to see how many of their friends they can spot. Alternatively play capture the flag (see page 40).

MANHUNT

Send someone off through the woods, dragging a stick behind them to leave a trail (see page 120). They should find a place to hide while the children rush off to find them. This is even more fun if played at night, but be sure to insist that the children stay with a partner at all times.

Safety tips

- **Make sure there are plenty of adults around to supervise.**
- **When using knives, follow the tool safety tips on page 156.**
- **For paintballing and flour bomb ambushes, provide safety goggles to protect players' eyes.**
- **After using flour grenades, collect all the paper and leave the woods as you found them.**

CAMPING PARTIES

Children love sleeping outdoors for a night, whether in the back garden or out in the wilderness. Telling scary stories and toasting marshmallows round an open fire, and then sleeping beneath the stars and waking to freshly cooked bacon butties, is a thrilling adventure and a great way to share time together outside.

OUTDOOR SLEEPOVERS

One of our most memorable parties was a December camping trip for eight-year-old boys. There were some rather anxious parents who dropped their children off that chilly, dark afternoon, wondering where on earth we were going, but there was no trepidation as far as the boys were concerned. Instead of using torches we relied on our night sight to follow a 3.25km/2-mile trail through the woods to a small barn. The children believed they were intrepid explorers entering the unknown, but in fact we had driven there earlier to deliver supplies. Amazing things happen when children are out at night: even the toughest refuses to go to the back of the line and they all stick close to the adults and become less boisterous. They spent most of the night huddled around a stove telling ghost stories and being rude, as boys (and dads) do so well. Having arrived in the dark, they had no idea where they were, and there was much excitement when they woke up the next morning to find themselves in a magical frosty wonderland. All survived to tell the tale of their adventure, which many are still telling ten years on.

On another occasion we took some young teenage girls to a remote rural site with no flushing toilets, no running water and nowhere to plug in a hair dryer. To make things even worse, we confiscated all portable DVD players, phones and other electrical equipment. But the complaining soon stopped when they realized they could have just as much fun making their own entertainment. The forest at night can be very noisy and one ghost story was punctuated by the screams of a muntjac deer, making it unforgettable.

TIPS FOR CAMPING PARTIES

● Find a good place to camp, whether it's the back garden, a local farm or a campsite. Always get permission to camp wild.

● Make sure everyone brings a really warm sleeping bag and extra clothes.

● You don't need a tent: sleeping out under the stars on a fine clear night is wonderful. Or try making your own shelter.

● Take a few treats such as marshmallows and games such as glow sticks (see page 56).

OUTDOOR FEASTS

Many children never cook for themselves, so find it a thrill to prepare their own meal out in the woods and cook it over a campfire. Or how about waking up after a sleepover and making breakfast over the embers of a fire? These children loved frying their own eggs and bacon. If you can't go to the woods, use a fire pan or an upturned metal dustbin lid to make a confined fire in the garden.

WILD FOOD HUNT

There are some rather grown-up boys who still talk about this particular party and it changed one lad's life forever. Everyone dressed up as savages, camouflaging themselves with face paint, leaves and twigs. They each found a long straight stick, stripped off the bark and sharpened one end to make a spear. They were split into small groups and sent along a woodland trail to find food for their supper, going quietly to avoid scaring off the game. At various points along the trail they found carrots, potatoes, swedes, turnips and even some dead pigeons and a pheasant (obtained from our local butcher) strung between the trees. Each child had to hit the food with their spear before carrying it off for their team.

Having sought permission from a local farmer we had established a safe area for lighting fires. Each team was challenged to light a small fire, just big enough to cook on, and then make a tasty stew from the scavenged ingredients. The biggest challenge was preparing the vegetables and meat – the children certainly learnt where meat comes from. But no one refused to prepare the pigeons and even the vegetarian turned into a meat eater. There was a tasting competition, with a prize for the best stew, and every single plate was licked clean. If we had served turnip and pigeon stew at home I'm sure none of those children would have touched it.

Safety tips

- **Observe the tool safety and fire safety tips on page 156.**
- **Make sure children wash their hands before preparing and eating food.**

ACTIVE ADVENTURE PARTIES

ROUTE MARCH AND ASSAULT COURSE

One chilly December day we held an army party. We invited children to come with camouflage clothing and a backpack, and issued everyone with a ration box of party food before setting out in pairs on a long route march. The sergeant major made up marching chants to keep the troops in time, which the troops echoed ('We all know that Ben's the best, he will never let us rest'). No one seemed to notice the driving frozen sleet. Every now and again parents ambushed the unsuspecting troops with flour bombs. When we reached a woodland glade, we sat on the frozen ground to eat the rations, warming our hands around mugs of tea made in a Kelly kettle. The journey back involved balancing along logs, crawling under an old tarpaulin, using a rope swing to cross a stream and climbing over a fallen tree, so everyone had warmed up by the time we got home.

ANIMAL SAFARI AND TRACKING

The invitation promised an adventure to track lion and rhinoceros in deepest, darkest Africa; the children had to wear green or brown clothes and bring binoculars (if they had them). We borrowed a Land Rover and drove off to the African plains, stopping now and again to follow tracks (fake ones laid in advance) through the woods, trying to find the elusive animals. Through binoculars the children spotted a lion and a rhinoceros in the distance (two parents who, unbeknown to the children, had been persuaded to dress up). Then it was tracking games and tag in the fields, followed by a safari tea.

For more ideas on tracking and stalking games, see pages 107–33.

STRAW BALE PARTY

We have had several great parties with a few small straw bales bought from a local farmer, who kindly delivered them and picked them up afterwards. We used the bales to make a pirate ship for a pirate party, a fort for an army party and two bases for flour bomb fights, and for playing team games promoting strategy and communication. If you have the space to do this, try contacting local farmers or searching on the Internet for a source of small traditional straw bales.

STRAW BALE OBSTACLE COURSE

Place the bales like stepping stones, but too far apart for it to be possible to jump from one to the other. Then place ladders or smaller stepping-stones between some of them. Start two teams off from different ends and provide each with a plank to use for crossing the gaps. Can they complete the course without stepping on the grass? If anyone steps off the bales or planks, they have to go back to the beginning. This game is great fun, especially when the teams pass in the middle.

TIPS FOR OUTDOOR PARTIES

● Be prepared for all eventualities. Make sure everyone dresses appropriately for the time of year and weather conditions.

● Don't just have an ordinary party tea. Prepare ration boxes for an expedition or a feast for fairies, or supplement your meal with some natural foraging. Or how about a scavenger hunt to find the party tea?

● Add a sense of adventure and magic. The children need to believe they are going off for a real adventure, and that they might find scary creatures or magical fairies. Make the local woods or the park special and exciting by pretending you are off to discover uncharted territory, find another planet, or spy on fierce dinosaurs or shy fairies. Add to the excitement and mystery by blindfolding the children before leading them into the woods or making a trail for them to follow to a secret destination.

● Make a wild birthday cake. Some friends celebrate every birthday with spectacular cakes decorated with flowers and wild fruits according to the season. If you do this, be sure to use non-poisonous plants.

● Be equipped. Always take a first-aid kit, sunscreen, drinks, food and some extra clothes. A tarpaulin comes in handy as an emergency shelter.

● Enlist plenty of adult help. Choose parents who are big kids and will join in with the adventure. Ensure there is a high ratio of adults to children.

● Go for safety in numbers. Make sure children stay in pairs or teams. It is also a good idea to establish a camp in a central and obvious location. Let the children run around and let off steam, but always make it clear where the limits are.

WILD GAMES

WILD GAMES

When choosing a school for our children, we decided against judging each one on its glossy prospectus, its reported academic achievements or the standard of its buildings. Instead we wandered through playgrounds at break time. We saw bleak tarmac spaces, full of bored children standing around aimlessly, hands thrust deep in their pockets. Eventually we found a school where the playground was a hive of activity: balls flew everywhere, and children ran, skipped, jumped or were embroiled in intense negotiations for prize marbles. This was obviously the place for our children.

There's nothing like adventurous play in playgrounds, gardens and green spaces for making children feel happy and free, for developing confidence and team playing, and for fine-tuning risk-assessing skills. And of course outdoor games burn off calories and get rid of frustrations, enabling better concentration. Children neither want nor need to be mollycoddled, wrapped up in cotton wool and told not to play conkers or lively ball games. Let them play wild games and scrape their knees; let them get a bit grubby; let them climb trees and explore the woods; let them chase and hide.

Despite what the advertisers tell us, it isn't necessary to buy expensive plastic toys or complicated gadgets to have fun. Give children the freedom to discover their own resourcefulness, test their imaginations and work together as a team to make up new games. They may even find that inventing their own versions of games is more fun.

OLD FAVOURITES

The best games are those that can be adapted for different situations and numbers of children. Don't feel obliged to stick to rules that don't suit your circumstances; be flexible and invent your own version. But make sure everyone knows the rules before you start.

CAPTURE THE FLAG

An enduringly popular game with scout groups and in school playgrounds. All you need is two teams, a couple of flags and an outdoor space. Although suitable for playing anywhere, it is probably most fun in woods where there are lots of places to hide. There are different versions of the game, but the basic rules are as follows.

- Hide the flags. Add to the challenge by making each team locate hidden flags using clues, grid references, bearings or perhaps photographs, or try texting clues to mobile phones.

- Play with several flags. Whichever team captures the most flags within a certain time is the winner.

- Place a flag on someone. Then track him or her down, as in a manhunt.

- Attach the flag to an object or ball. Once captured, it can be thrown to other team members.

- Be adaptable. Use whatever is available wherever you are and make up your own version for however many people are there at the time.

How to play

- First make your flags. Make them in advance or improvise with a bandana, a T-shirt or even a large leaf on a stick.

- Make two teams, each with their own territory, divided by a natural boundary such as a path, a stream or a row of trees. If there is no obvious boundary, mark one with smaller flags or sticks. Designate an area within each territory as a jail.

- Each team places their flag in their territory, in a spot visible to the other team. The aim of the game is to sneak in to the other team's territory, steal their flag and carry it across to home territory without being tagged.

- Anyone caught by a member of the other team is either out of the game or has to go to jail until released by a team member, depending on what has been agreed at the beginning of the game.

- If the person who has stolen the flag is tagged while running back to their home territory, the flag must be returned to base.

- A team can claim victory only when they have placed the other team's flag within their own territory.

FORTY-FORTY

As children we loved the excitement of playing forty-forty in the local farmyard, hiding among the old buildings and then racing to reach the base before being caught.

How to play
● Play in an open space surrounded by potential hiding places, such as a woodland clearing or a park with plenty of trees and bushes.
● Establish a base in the middle of the clearing – a tree or bush, or marked with a log. Make sure everyone knows where the base is.
● Select someone as seeker. They sit at the base, shut their eyes and count to forty twice while everyone else dashes off to hide around the edge of the clearing.
● The seeker calls out 'Forty-forty coming, ready or not' and then looks for the hiders while keeping an eye on the base, which the hiders try to reach without being seen or caught.
● Any hiders managing to sneak to the base without being spotted or tagged call out 'Forty-forty home'.
● The last person to be tagged becomes the seeker in the next game.

KICK THE CAN

Dig out a can from your recycling bin and have a go at kick the can, which is another version of forty-forty. Follow the rules for forty-forty, but instead of establishing a base place a can in the middle and choose an area to be a jail. When the seeker or 'it' sees a hider, they have to race them back to the can; if 'it' gets there first, he or she yells out the name and location of the hider, who then goes to jail. If the hider gets to the can first, they can kick it and release their fellow hiders from jail.

BRITISH BULLDOG

Banned by some schools as far too rough, this wild game remains a children's favourite. It's all about a headlong dash towards your friends, dodging grasping hands so that you can run to safety at the other end of a field.

How to play
● Select one or two people as 'bulldogs' to stand in the middle of an open space.
● Everyone else (the runners) stands at one end and at a pre-arranged signal tries to run to the other end (home) without getting caught by a bulldog.
● If a bulldog catches a runner and holds them long enough to shout 'British bulldog, one, two, three', the runner becomes a bulldog.
● In a less boisterous version, the bulldogs simply tag the runners rather than trying to grab hold of them.
● The first two or the last two caught become the bulldogs in the next game.

DODGE BALL

Similar to British bulldog, but instead of runners being tagged a ball is thrown at them. Use a slightly soft football or volleyball if playing with young children; older ones prefer to play with a harder, faster ball.

Some basic dodge ball rules
● One or two people stand in the centre of an open space, armed with a ball.
● Everyone else lines up at one end of the open space and then tries to run to the other end without being 'tagged' by a ball.
● If the ball hits you, you are out of the game, unless you catch the ball.

FRENCH CRICKET

This favourite family game is perfect for any number of people at parties and gatherings on the beach, at the park or in the garden. All you need is a small ball (a tennis ball is ideal) and a bat: this might be a cricket bat, but we have also used old tennis rackets and rounders bats. To make it a real challenge, our boys once used a thin wooden sword; they have also used driftwood on the beach and a stick in the woods.

How to play

- One batsman stands in the middle of an open playing area. Everyone else stands around them in a large circle.
- The aim is to get the batsman out by catching them out or hitting them below the knee with the ball.
- Someone starts off by throwing the ball at the batsman, keeping it below knee level.
- Wherever the ball lands up – whether it is hit by the batsman or not – someone else goes to the ball and then throws it from that spot.
- Keep playing until the batsman is out. Let everyone have a go at batting.

Variations

- Decide whether or not the batsman can move his or her feet. We usually say they have to keep their feet in the same place unless they hit the ball, in which case they may turn and face the next bowler.
- If the batsman hits the ball and it bounces, the fielders are only allowed to catch it in one hand. One hand, one bounce.
- Try the 'lunge' rule. The batsman holds his (or her) bat at arm's length and turns 360 degrees to indicate his safe zone. If he thinks any fielder comes into this zone during the game, he can challenge him by shouting 'Lunge'; if he reaches out with his bat and touches the fielder he gains a life.

NATURAL VERSIONS OF TRADITIONAL GAMES

While we were staying at a remote camp miles from anywhere in the Okavango Delta in Botswana, the adults would rest during the midday heat, but the children began to get itchy feet. With no electricity and no games, there were only books and sketchbooks for entertainment. But one day the camp manager collected some large round seeds about the size of tennis balls and challenged the children to a game of 'bush boules', which they played in an open area of sand. The competition was fierce and before long even the resting adults were tempted to joined in. Wherever you are, you will be able to find natural and recycled materials which you can use as props and equipment to bring your own slant to traditional games.

RECYCLED SKITTLES

The contents of the average recycling bin offer all sorts of possibilities for improvised games. We made our own version of skittles by filling empty plastic drinks bottles with coloured water and using a cricket ball to knock them over. No need to pay a fortune at the bowling alley: just get some mates together and play at home.

AUNT SALLY

Many parts of the world have their own distinctive local games; Aunt Sally is popular in our area. Dating back to the seventeenth century and traditionally played in pubs and at fairgrounds, it involves throwing sticks to knock a skittle (called a dolly) off a metal pole. Have a go at making your own version out of pieces of collected wood.

What you need
- An open space, away from anything that might be broken or damaged by flying sticks
- A long stick
- 6 throwing sticks, roughly 45cm/18in long and 5cm/2in in diameter
- 1 thicker piece of wood, about 1m/3ft long and carved to a point at one end – we improvised and used the heavy metal base of a shade umbrella as a post
- 1 dolly – improvise by using a ball or carve a skittle from wood

Safety tips

- **All players should stand well behind the line and watch out for flying sticks.**
- **Do not attempt to retrieve sticks until the end of a round.**

How to play
- Lay the long stick on the ground to make a line about 10m/30ft from the post. Each player stands behind this when playing. Although the official throwing distance is 10m/30ft, use whatever distance is appropriate for the ages of the children playing.
- Bang the thicker piece of wood into the ground until the top is about 75cm/30in above ground level. Balance the dolly on top of the post.
- Decide how many rounds you will play.
- Each player gets six throws per round. Sticks must be thrown underarm.
- If the dolly is knocked down, it must be put back on the post straight away.
- The person who hits the dolly off the post the most times is the winner.

QUOITS

The traditional game involves throwing metal rings over a metal pin; other versions use wooden or even rope rings. We played with woven willow rings.

What you need
- A sharpened stick (the pin), pushed into the ground
- 4 sticks, each about 50cm/20in long, laid out in a square around the pin
- 4 quoits – we made ours by twisting bendy green willow and hazel stems into circles

How to play
- Choose the throwing distance according to the age of the group and weight of the quoits, and then mark the playing position with a long stick.
- Each player throws four quoits in a round.
- Throwing a quoit over the pin counts as two points. If a quoit falls beside the pin but within the square, that is worth one point.
- Choose a number of points to aim for before the game – first to twenty, perhaps.

WILD MARBLES

Like most young boys, Edward had a marble craze. He collected marbles of all colours and sizes, squirrelling them away and bringing them out now and again to sort and admire them, and play games with them. His marbles were made of brightly coloured glass, but the earliest marbles, used by the children of ancient Egypt and pre-Christian Rome, were probably spherical pebbles or balls of clay. Encourage children to look for natural spheres such as round pebbles, crab apples, oak apple galls and conkers, or roll wild clay into small balls and let it dry naturally. Then try a few wild marble games with friends out in the woods, at the beach or in the garden:

- **Circle game** Draw a circle in bare soil or sand. Place a wild marble in the centre and then try to knock it out of the circle using the other marbles.
- **Marble golf** Poke a small hole in the ground or in sand and see who can roll their marbles into the hole.

INVENTING OUTDOOR GAMES

Whenever our children were at a loose end they used to wander down the road and see which neighbours were in. They would invariably find someone to play with and would often make up a new game. The starting point was usually something they found lying around, perhaps an old hula hoop or a punctured rugby ball. Over the years they invented games to play with two children or a crowd, games for mixed age groups and games adapted for large and small gardens – often with fiercely contested rules.

Back in the year 2000 a friend was asked to organize a game for his local fête. Not being one to stick with convention, he decided to invent something new. He found an old frisbee and some quoits in the back of the garage, and came up with Millennium Celebrity Frisbee Quoits. I have no idea what was involved, but it proved the most popular attraction at the fête

and the competition lasted all afternoon.

Wherever you are, have some fun by thinking outside the box and using whatever you can find to make up your own weird and wonderful games, whether based on old favourites or something entirely new. Here are a few games our children and their friends have invented over the years.

HOOP BALL

Cliffie and Frankie combined netball and rugby and came up with hoop ball, the perfect game for a small garden. Any size of ball will do, but a mini basketball is perfect.

How to play

● Any number of players can join in, split into two teams.

● Hang a hula hoop (or large willow ring) on a branch at each end of a garden or open space. If there are no trees, you may have to come up with another plan. The aim is to score points by throwing the ball through the other side's hoop.

● Mark out a penalty box below each hoop with sticks.

● You may run with the ball but can't enter the penalty area while holding it.

● You can throw the ball to team members standing within the penalty area. You can only shoot from within the penalty area.

● What makes this game exciting is that you can make rugby-style low-body tackles but you cannot snatch the ball. The only way to get the ball from the other team is to intercept passes or pick it up when an opponent drops it after being tackled or fumbling a pass.

● Cliffie and Frankie warn that this can be a rough game. However, as with rugby, there is an alternative touch version: if tagged you must give the ball to the opposition.

KNEE VOLLEYBALL

The perfect game when little children are playing with older ones: everyone is on their knees, so they are all equally disadvantaged! Mark out a rough court with a spade, sticks or some rope and make a line on the ground to represent a net. Follow the same rules as for normal volleyball, hitting or throwing the ball over the line. This game is great fun, but very hard on the knees and the jeans!

EGGY

This is a good playground game, suitable for up to ten players. You need a wall with a hard surface around it, suitable for bouncing a tennis or squash ball on.

How to play

● If there are 10 players, each one draws a lot to be allocated a number from 1 to 10. Using their hand as a racket, each player hits the ball against the wall in number order.

● If a player misses the ball, doesn't hit the wall or hits it after two bounces, they lose a life and move down to the position of the bottom number (position 10). Everyone else's number order then changes, so take care to keep track of whose turn it is.

● If you lose a life at position 10 you are out of the game. Remaining players must remember the new order, 9 now being the last number.

● The winner is the last person left in.

BUM'S UP!

This is always a favourite, perhaps because of the name. Play only with a soft ball and nowhere near any windows (Ed, I hope you're feeling guilty if you're reading this!). For an extra challenge, use a water-filled balloon instead of a ball.

How to play

● Everyone stands in a circle. One person throws or kicks the ball to someone else. They then throw or kick it to another person in the circle, and so on.

● If a person doesn't catch the ball, they lose a life and go down on one knee. If they fail to catch the ball the next time it is thrown to them, they go down on two knees; lose another life and they have to catch the next ball with one hand. If they lose this life, they must go and face a wall or fence with their bottom up.

● Everyone else takes turns to kick the ball at the backside of the poor person against the wall. If anyone misses, they also become a target. The game usually ends up with a line of bums against the wall and one delighted victor!

THE STICK TOWER CHALLENGE

Who can make the tallest freestanding tower using only sticks and string? The teenagers didn't look at all keen on this idea, but once they got started the precariously balanced towers grew taller and taller; no one wanted to admit defeat! This game is great fun and also helps develop communication, team building and problem solving. Play with two or more teams with up to five players in each team. Provide each team with a ball of string and about twenty straight sticks, all cut to the same length.

BEACH GAMES

Stuck at the beach with no games in sight? Have a look around and see what you can find. Jake and Dan made a cricket bat and a rounders bat from driftwood. Having no ball, they tried using a round pebble, but soon realized this wasn't such a good idea, so they cut an old tyre into strips and wound these together to make a rough-and-ready ball. Here are some other games you could play at the beach.

STONE PICTURES

The Victoria and Albert Museum in London has been running a long-term international art project called the World Beach Project, which encourages people to make stone pictures, patterns and sculptures on a beach, photograph their creation with a digital camera and submit the pictures to the project through the V&A website. The project is a perfect way to link natural exploration and creativity with modern technology. If you wish to enter it, go to the V&A website (www.vam.ac.uk) to find out more. Or try making stone pictures at your favourite beach and then taking digital photographs to place on the school website or on your social networking page.

STONE JENGA

The game of Jenga (from kujenga, a Swahili verb meaning to build) involves building a tower of wooden blocks and then removing a block at a time, the challenge being to leave the tower standing for as long as possible. This beach version involves building a tower of small stones. Each person takes it in turn to add a stone to the top of the tower; if your stone makes the tower collapse you are the loser. If you play with larger stones, great care is needed: you don't want the stones to tumble on top of you. To make the game more fun, allow each person to stabilize the top stone by inserting smaller pebbles beneath it before they add their own stone to the top of the tower.

THE STONE TOWER CHALLENGE

Each person searches the beach for flat stones and then very carefully builds a tower, using as many stones as they possibly can. Can anyone beat Bridget's record of sixteen stones in a single tower?

Safety tips

- **Stone towers can easily collapse, so build with care on a firm, level base.**

SKIMMING STONES

The World Skimming Championship is held each year on the Scottish island of Easdale. Each competitor is allowed five skims and the stone must bounce on the water at least three times. Can you beat the world record of forty bounces?

How to play

● All you need is a source of flat oval or spherical pebbles and a body of water. Take a stone and throw it across the water, flicking the wrist so that it is thrown almost horizontally and skips across the surface of the water without sinking.

● The aim is to make the stone skip as far as possible. Count the number of skims or estimate the distance the stone travels before sinking.

● Try out different versions of the game. For instance, can you make your stones jump over a log or rock in the water?

NIGHT GAMES

When darkness falls children usually disappear indoors and shut out the night. Yet darkness can offer excitement, inspiration and fun, from star gazing and looking for nocturnal wildlife to playing night games. Let children discover the wonders of the night and experience the real darkness that so many of us never see. A good starting point is playing games together after dark.

Safety tips

- **When playing night games, make sure that all children are paired with a buddy, and keep doing regular head counts to make sure no one has got lost.**
- **If using glow sticks, collect them when the game is over and take them home.**

NIGHT FORTY-FORTY

Similar to normal forty-forty (see page 43) but whoever is 'it' tries to catch people by shining a torch beam on them and calling out 'Forty-forty, I see Robert', or whatever their name is. That person is duly out. For an added challenge, blindfold the seeker and play the game using sounds as well.

GLOW-STICK GAMES

Glow sticks, available from good toyshops, are perfect for using in all sorts of games after dark. We have laid glow-stick trails for night treasure hunts, made them into lanterns for night walks, decorated ourselves for glowing night dances and played glow-stick rugby with a ball made from an old plastic drink bottle containing water and glow sticks. Or how about taping a couple of glow sticks to your frisbee?

NIGHT CAPTURE THE FLAG

Playing as explained on page 40, decorate flags with luminous pens to make them visible at night. Or make a flag from glow sticks. Or play in the dark without torches and rely on your night vision.

BUBBLE GAMES

In November 2007 Samsam Bubbleman enclosed fifty people within a single bubble. As if this wasn't amazing enough, he won another record for putting an astonishing sixty-six bubbles inside one single bubble. Mix your own bubble mixture and then go outdoors on a still day to try making enormous rainbow-coloured bubbles. It is guaranteed to get children jumping off the sofa and out into the garden, whatever their age. Eighteen-year-old Jake, seven-year-old Anya and I were all totally engrossed when we tried this out for ourselves.

You will need
- Detergent or shampoo (see below)
- Softened water, distilled water or rainwater
- Glycerine
- A large shallow container – a baking tray or roasting pan is ideal
- 2 x 20cm/8in straws (short enough to fit in the container) and some cotton string

Basic bubble recipes
In any quantity to the ratio:

- 1 part Johnson's Baby Shampoo/1 part water/¼ part glycerine
- Or: 3 parts Johnson's Baby Shampoo/1 part water/¼ part glycerine – a thick gloopy mixture if bubbles need to withstand a slight wind
- Or: 1 part green Fairy Liquid/8 parts water/1 part glycerine

Mix all the ingredients together gently in your container. If foam accumulates, scoop it off. Allow the mixture to stand overnight, or for as long as the children will wait!

Making the wand

The best way to make large bubbles is with a flexible, adjustable string-and-straw wand. Thread a length of cotton string through two straws, tying the ends together to make a circle. Slide the knot into the middle of one of the straws.

Making giant bubbles

- Pour the solution into the shallow container.
- Dip the wand into the solution until the string is completely soaked. Hold one straw and slowly pull it out of the solution. Gently pull the wand through the air to form a long snake-like bubble.
- To cut your bubble off, tilt the straw to close the gap between the strings.
- Keep practising until you get the knack.
- Keep any leftover solution for another day.

Trapping someone inside a bubble

For a real challenge, pour bubble solution into an upturned dustbin lid, placed on some bricks to make it stable. Ask a small child to stand in the solution and then, using a straw-and-string wand as above, try to pull a bubble up over their head.

Bubble tips

- **Weather** The best bubbles are made on still humid days (after rain is perfect, or in the morning or evening). If the weather is hot and dry, add more glycerine; if it's windy, make a stronger solution.
- **Type of soap/detergent** We found that Johnson's Baby Shampoo was excellent, also Fairy washing-up liquid (green, not yellow). We have heard that Joy, Dawn or Persil's Aloe Vera, washing-up liquids also work well.
- **Glycerine** This helps soap bubbles retain water. You can buy it from any pharmacist's shop.
- **Age of the mixture** If you can persuade the children to wait, the best bubbles are made from a mixture left for at least two hours or even overnight.
- **Ratio of water : detergent : glycerine** This is vital. See the recipes above, but do experiment.
- **Foam** is the enemy of bubbles. If it forms in your tray, scoop it away immediately.

WILD STORIES

WILD STORYTELLING

STORYBOARDS AND STORY PICTURES

WILD POETRY, CHARMS AND SPELLS

STORY STICKS

WILD STORIES

There must have been at least 200 people there that night, yet the only sounds were the crackle of the fire and the ebb and flow of the storyteller's lilting voice. Rapt faces glowed in the blaze, adults and children watching and listening as Jeremy Hastings wove together the disparate threads of a magical tale.

This story was determined partly by the audience, for at each critical point he invited suggestions. What was the heroine called? What was she like? Where did she live? What did she want? Jeremy had stipulated that the story needed a hero and a heroine and had to finish right there by the fire, but the rest was up to the audience.

The resulting tale involved a wheelchair-bound 125-year-old woman who lived in a tree house on the other side of the world, and her crazy adventures with an equally unlikely hero; it finished rather dramatically with them both falling into the fire. 'But,' said Jeremy, his figure almost ghostly in the flickering fire-light, 'their spirits now dwell within the trees all around this place. I've never heard a story like that before. This is your story.' It was pure theatre.

Other storytellers took to the stage that night. Some were funny, some were musical and some told sinister tales that sent shivers down the spine. Who needs TV or computer games when you can have entertainment like this?

Stories have the power to engage and inspire, and telling them in a wild setting adds another dimension, for the natural world adds atmosphere and provides stimulation for the imagination. Wild stories are a magical way to bring people together and for families and groups to share each other's company in the great outdoors. Nature can inspire or provide the materials for the creation of pictures, poems and spells as well.

WILD STORYTELLING

Stories are all around us – in newspapers, books, on TV and on the Internet – but storytelling only happens when the story is passed directly from person to person, without the use of print or technology. We all have stories within us, and storytelling is a way for young people to invent their own non-electronic virtual worlds and develop open-ended tales. It's also an opportunity to imagine the world from another perspective – that of an animal, perhaps, or a tree or even a rock.

For ancient peoples one of the purposes of storytelling was to pass information on to the next generation about how to survive and live with nature. Today it is still a wonderful and enjoyable way to teach young people about the natural world and their place within it.

Outdoor stories need a few vital ingredients to flourish and grow: an inspiring setting, a receptive audience and a few props to release the imagination. Here are some ideas.

The setting
- What mood do you wish to create? Choose somewhere atmospheric – perhaps a woodland clearing, a hidden valley, an open hilltop or a place beneath the spreading branches of a large tree. If telling stories after dark, find somewhere away from bright lights.
- Be inspired by miniature landscapes, such as a gnarled old tree stump where fairies might live, or by giant landscapes where giants might roam.
- A fire can be a wonderful focus, whether a bonfire out in the wilderness or a small pit fire or a barbecue in the back garden on a summer's night. See the fire safety tips on page 156.

A storytelling throne

A decorated throne brings a sense of occasion to any gathering, including one for storytelling. Create one by adorning a tree stump with branches and greenery or weaving grasses and leaves through an outdoor chair.

Setting a story rolling

To stimulate storytelling, provide a few props, beat a rhythm, dress up in costumes, do something different. Here are a few ideas to break the ice and get a story started:

● To engage your audience, consider who they are and what kind of tale might entice them in. Storytelling is as much about the art of listening as telling, and of course the listeners' role is then to pass the story on to others. Perhaps one person could tell a story of their own or seek details from the audience. Or perhaps a whole group could be involved in a shared story that passes on from one person to the next.

● Seek inspiration from nature, perhaps viewing it from different and unusual perspectives. Visit wild places at night or as the sun is rising; go out in a wild wind or the swirling fog. Try melting into a place to search for its stories by sitting quietly on your own: what can you see, hear and feel?

● Don't try to be formulaic or guide anyone too much; people are more likely to be creative if left to their own devices. Just provide a starting point and see where it takes them. The best stories are often the simplest ones.

● Remember the power of scary stories: everyone loves a bit of spine-tingling excitement.

● Use characters from a favourite storybook as a starting point, but take them off on some completely new adventures.

● Try to see the world from another point of view. Who lives out there in the woods, for instance? How do they see the world? How do they see us?

● Ask everyone to sit in a circle, facing outwards with their eyes shut. What is the first thing they see when they open their eyes? Can you use this in a story?

● Pretend to be reporters and make a story from your interviews with natural characters you find. What is it like to live in a burrow? What did the crabby hawthorn tree have to say? What did he think of the cheeky robin who lived in his branches?

everyone to take an object out of the bag and incorporate it into his or her own story or a shared tale.

Story collections

Before the storytelling begins, invite everyone to collect a few loose natural materials from the surrounding area. Challenge each person to weave his or her natural collection into a story. Or do a sensory scavenger hunt to discover wet grass, slimy mud, cool wind, soft moss, prickly thorns, bringing out vivid descriptive words to use in the storytelling.

Masks, puppets and teddy bears

Even the shyest storyteller might get involved through using natural masks (see page 82) or puppets (see page 90). Or how about taking a favourite teddy or soft toy to the woods for an adventure and photographing it in different places to inspire a story, either outdoors or back in the classroom?

Mystery creatures

A wonderful way to get the story juices flowing is to make little people or creatures from lumps of clay, twigs and seeds or whatever you can find. Where might these characters live? What do they eat? Who are their enemies? What adventures might they have?

Telling the tale

The best storytellers use voice and movement to bring their characters alive.

● Don't be tempted to shout; a soft voice draws an audience gently into a tale. Let the voice ebb and flow, vary the pitch and tone, and give each character a distinctive sound.

● Be prepared to be silly and act the clown, or to make your voice sinister and haunting – whatever your tale requires.

● Use rhythm and repetition to strengthen a story. After a while the audience will probably join in.

● Be larger than life: use big movements to add drama and spectacle if need be.

A storyteller's charm

A sea-sculpted stone, a special shell or a beautiful feather can make a storyteller's charm. Choose something tactile, unusual and intriguing. Pass the charm around the circle until the leader says stop; whoever is holding the charm becomes the storyteller.

A story bag

Fill a bag or basket with natural materials or objects made from natural resources, such as shells, arrowheads, a chewed fir cone or nut, a feather, a wooden figure, a painted egg or perhaps a little bottle for potions or spells. Invite

Sound effects and musical instruments

We remember storyteller Chris Holland telling a tale about an animal going off on a quest through the rainforest. Chris used movements and different voices to bring the characters alive, but it was his use of simple percussion instruments that really engaged the audience. Try making natural sound effects with stones, sticks or crackling leaves, or make your own percussion instruments (see page 101). Or how about asking each child to be a character with their own distinct sound?

Magic eyes

To inspire a story make cardboard eyes of different colours and shapes and, using double-sided sticky tape, stick them on to logs, twigs, trees or any other natural features to make all sorts of imaginary creatures. Alternatively, use chalk or charcoal to draw eyes on natural features. Are your creatures happy or sad? Why might they be feeling that way? Remember to take the card eyes home with you and to wipe off any chalk or charcoal marks.

Magnifying glasses

Encourage children to investigate small places with a magnifying glass and imagine what adventures might happen in the complex miniature worlds they discover. Perhaps they might crawl through the grass following an ant. Where does it go? Who does it meet? Afterwards gather everyone together to share the adventures they have imagined.

Word and picture pools

The most sparkling stories are full of vivid words that draw pictures in your mind. A word or picture pool is another great way to encourage descriptive language.

● Go out into the local park or woodland and find interesting natural materials to look at and touch, and collect them in a goody bag. Or take everyone on a blindfold walk to explore through touch. Or encourage each person to sit alone somewhere, become immersed in the natural world and jot down words and feelings, or think about the animals that might live there.

● Bring everyone together and, using water-soluble pens, chalk or charcoal, write words or draw pictures on fallen leaves or smooth pebbles. Put all the words and images together in a 'pool'.

● As the story is told, each person pulls a leaf or stone from the pool, incorporating the word or picture into the story.

STORYBOARDS AND STORY PICTURES

The magic of favourite storybooks is often in the pictures more than the words. Have a go at making wild pictures using loose natural materials in the woods or at the beach. You can use these to illustrate or inspire wild stories, or you can create a series of pictures to make a storyboard.

This beach storyboard tells the tale of a surfer waiting in front of a fire for just the right wave. Eventually the perfect wave arrives and he has the ride of his life, unaware of the enormous shark lurking beneath the water waiting to gobble him up. The story finishes with a happy smiling shark. The storyboard attracted the attention from a passing family, who stopped to add to the story.

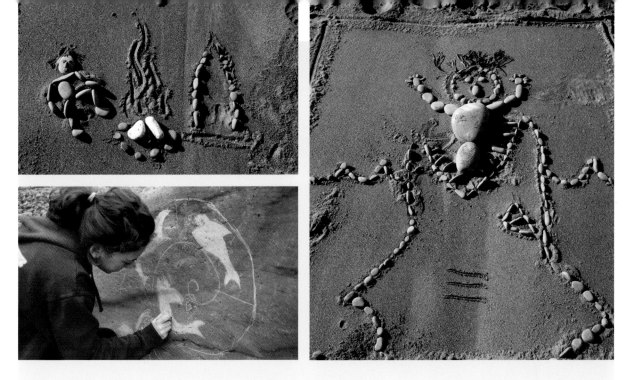

Other story pictures made that day included a pebble and seaweed lion made by Jake, while Rebecca found a wave-smoothed rock on which, using a soft pebble, she drew a story about a mermaid and a friendly dolphin, following the contours in a spiral. The fact that her drawing would be washed clean by the incoming tide made the story more powerful, catching the mood of the moment.

The starting point for the woodland pictures below was memories. After sharing memories of outdoor experiences, we wove some of our favourites into pictures made from natural materials. There is an owl in a tree with the moon and stars, and a dragon lurking near by. Another picture showed a farmyard scene complete with chickens, a tractor and this beautiful red fox.

WILD POETRY, CHARMS AND SPELLS

The wildness of a storm, the beauty of daffodils, the loneliness of the sea – poets have always been inspired by nature. Go outdoors and encourage children to slow down, look around and free their imaginations. Perhaps they could lie on the forest floor and look up into the leaf canopy, or peer into the depths of a pond to discover a tadpole's world. Or hang leaves from a tree and listen as the wind jostles and plays with them. What must it be like to be a tiny insect crawling around in a flower or a bird soaring up among the clouds? Help the children use their experiences creatively, for instance by writing poetry. Below are some other ideas.

Ideas for finding wild inspiration

● Instead of writing an ordinary poem, how about making up a spell? Add a pinch of the scent of the apple blossom, a pearl of the dew from a spider's web, a rush of wind from the tree tops, a splash of the deepest ruby red they can find and hair from the head of a woodland sprite. Or create a witch's brew, a charm or a magical potion.

● Go on a scavenger hunt to collect ingredients for a magic potion – perhaps scented leaves or fallen petals. Mix a potion in a pot and sprinkle it on imaginary creatures, or on puppets to bring them to life. Or just let the words fly out of your wand as a spell that turns other children into woodland creatures or mythical beasts.

● Create a word pool or story bag, as described on pages 66 and 67, and then ask each child to pull out some words or objects and try to incorporate them in a poem or spell. Or ask each child to write a single word on a leaf, using descriptive words as well as nouns, and then pin the leaves to a tree with black-thorn pins so that you can keep changing the order: for example, glittering water, lashing rain, glittering rain, smooth water, smooth leaves, lashing leaves.

● Connie found a lump of slate on the beach and decided to use it as a tablet, scratching down a few words on it with a small stone. Try using other novel ways of writing, in mud or with mud, with berry paint or with charcoal pencils. Try not to make the writing permanent; the idea is to create ephemeral poems.

STORY STICKS

During their travels through the bush, Australian aborigines sometimes attached natural materials to sticks in chronological order. The materials might have represented creatures, plants and rocks or even experiences and feelings. These journey sticks were like maps, which helped the traveller to recount their journey to others. Some ancient peoples also used message sticks marked with a series of lines and dots to send news and invitations, while Native Americans used a decorated talking stick to identify who was allowed to speak during their council meetings.

A story stick like this can also help tell a story. By relating the materials to elements in the story it can inspire the story, encourage an audience to listen or help reluctant storytellers to participate. Or it can bring an outdoor play to life, perhaps acting as a prop for a character or a symbol of magic. Making a story stick can in

itself make a walk more exciting, providing an opportunity to seek out natural objects and create something beautiful with them. So take inspiration from ancient peoples and go outdoors and try making your own story stick, or any of the variations suggested below.

Making a story stick

● Find a special stick – perhaps it's the bark, the colour, the shape or where you find it that makes it special. Only collect sticks from the ground.

● Scrape off all or some of the bark if you wish.

● Look around for natural materials such as feathers, shells, seeds, leaves – what you use will depend on what you find and on what sort of stick you wish to make.

● Attach your finds to the stick using coloured wools, garden twine, elastic bands or double-sided sticky tape.

A SHAMAN'S STICK

Shamans mediate between our world and the spirit world. Associated with wild places, they are wise and otherworldly. To make a shaman's stick, use some of the following:

- **Bells** To clear the air
- **Feathers** Birds represent the shaman's spirit flight
- **Bones** For example, a rabbit's skull or leg bone, but only use bones bleached clean by the sun. Shamans believe bones have the power to channel the spirit
- **Natural colours** For example, squashed berries, crushed chalk or charcoal, to paint on patterns

A FAIRY WAND

Attach pretty things such as honesty seeds, white feathers, flowers and fluffy clematis seeds to your stick. Decorate the tip with a bendy twig folded into a star.

A RAINBOW STICK

Wind a strip of double-sided sticky tape around a stick in a spiral and collect fragments of colour such as leaves or fallen petals to stick along the tape to make a rainbow effect.

A SCAVENGING STICK

Wind double-sided sticky tape around a stick and then attach treasures such as feathers, seeds and leaves to record a walk or start a story. If some things won't stick, try attaching them with twine or elastic bands. The children could pretend to be detectives solving a crime, searching for clues such as chewed nuts (why didn't the squirrel finish his nut?) or a lost feather (who lost it and why?). Add the clues to the scavenging sticks and then relate the story to the group afterwards.

WILD TRAILS

WILD TRAILS

A complex network of routes criss-crosses through the flower-rich chalk grassland, tangled scrub and dark, twisted yew trees of our local hillside. My goddaughter Eliza often drags her father up there to forge new trails and discover secret hideaways, where she makes camps and watches out for badgers and deer. I have seen how these adventures have helped her develop a sense of place, direction, observation and independence, making her more confident about exploring the countryside and more aware of natural signs.

This chapter is all about observing our surroundings through tracking, stalking and treasure hunts. It's about encouraging children to switch off virtual worlds and re-enter the real world and look at what is going on around them, whether walking through the park or even going on a car journey. By planning ahead, using maps and noticing what is around us, we can become much more tuned in to the wild world and enjoy observing its wonders at close quarters. Instead of two-dimensional virtual adventures in front of a screen indoors, try using the Internet, digital photography, mobile phones and global positioning systems (GPS) in real-life trail making to become more at home with wild places, enhance natural connections, heighten the senses and have some fun of a different kind.

So sharpen your eyes, tune in your ears and discover new places where you might get that prickling feeling at the nape of your neck and have some close encounters with wildlife.

WILD NAVIGATING

Would you be able to find your way in the wilderness without a map or compass? Anxious parents often won't let their offspring out of their sight, for fear that they wouldn't; but when our lives were closely intertwined with nature we found our way by using the sun, the moon, the stars, the weather, the landscape, plants, animals and plenty of common sense. So perhaps we should let children learn what they are capable of, by giving them opportunities to find their own way and even get a little lost. Try a few games to encourage navigation skills, heightened sensory awareness and a rudimentary understanding of maps.

NAVIGATING NATURALLY

If you were taken to an unfamiliar wild location and then taken for a short walk, would you be able to find your way back to the starting point? We usually rely on existing knowledge, someone else or a map; but what if you just have to rely on our powers of observation and what nature tells you?

Take a group of children on a short walk to a special place, asking them to take notice of things they see on the way, such as the direction of the sun, changes in vegetation, paths and tracks, distant landmarks. Then invite them to use these clues to find their way back to where they started; we have done this with our own children and they always find it easier than they expect, which gives them a real sense of achievement.

THE MAPPING GAME

Making a treasure map is an enjoyable way for children to learn how to get their bearings in an unfamiliar green space, as it encourages them to explore and look for natural features. Anya spent hours making this elaborate map of her garden, sticking sand on the paths and adding moss and flowers. She tested out her friends to see if they could find the hidden treasure, marked on the map with a red cross.

What you need

● White card, or paper clipped on to card from a cereal box
● Pencils, crayons and paints, including natural paints (see page 89)
● Glue
● Some kind of treasure, such as some tasty treats

Playing the mapping game

● Split the children into small groups and send them off to explore a defined area, which might include several trees or the corner of a meadow, or be as small as a tree stump or an anthill. Ask them to look for significant features such as footpaths and tracks, hedgerows, streams, ponds and trees, or, if the area is on a small scale, rabbit droppings, moss, flowers or nuts.
● Ask them to draw or paint a map showing how these features relate to each other.

● Each group then hides some treasure and marks the spot on their map. Perhaps they could gather some loose natural materials and stick them on to the map to provide a few more clues.
● Gather everyone back together and swap maps. Ask each group to find the treasure, using the map.
● Alternatively the children could find a special place to mark on the map and then ask the other group to find it and guess why that place is special.

FINDING YOUR WAY HOME

This game encourages using all the senses to find your way home after being blindfolded and taken on a short walk. Try it out with children in a familiar green space first until they are used to being blindfolded.

How to play

● Best played in an area of mixed habitats with tree cover and open spaces, and a range of ground surfaces, such as bare earth, stony paths, grassland and perhaps a woodland floor covered in dry twigs and leaves.

● Take a group of children to your chosen starting point and let them have a good look around. Ask each child to put on a blindfold.

Then hold hands in a line. Alternatively the children could work in pairs, with one as the leader and the other being blindfolded.

● Lead them on a short walk, encouraging them to use all their senses. Can they feel the direction of the sun and differences in temperature (woods, for instance, will be damper and cooler)? Perhaps they will feel what is under their feet (especially if they go barefoot!). Perhaps they will notice smells and sounds.

● When you have gone far enough, ask everyone to remove the blindfolds. Can they find their way back to the start, using common sense and natural navigation? Provide a few clues if necessary.

TRACKING AND STALKING

We followed in the tracker's footsteps as quietly as we could, looking around constantly, never knowing what we might see next. We had been following some massive paw prints, and now we were creeping very slowly round a large termite mound. Suddenly we saw her, strolling lazily towards the river, the low evening sunlight shining on her sleek golden coat. In all those miles of African bush our tracker, Judge, had found a lion. We felt privileged, humbled and a little fearful to see this majestic creature at such close quarters in the wild.

Becoming a tracker and stalker takes practice and an ability to read every natural sign. For ancient peoples the ability to find or avoid animals was not a luxury but the difference between life and death; today most of us spend much of our lives surrounded by man-made paraphernalia and have forgotten how to be close to nature. But by discovering how to read and understand natural signs you will be rewarded by the thrill of being able to observe wild animals and birds up close.

BECOMING A TRACKER

While sleeping out in the woods, a group of teenagers heard deer barking and a badger's pounding footsteps. Just imagine the excitement and thrill if they had actually seen these animals! If young people are to enjoy tracking, they have to believe they will see a fox around the corner or a deer over the hill. If you can keep them quiet, they just might be lucky.

After a particularly heavy fall of snow even the youngest child can have fun following animal tracks – finding where they go, trying to follow routes under fences and through hedges – and noticing other signs. Little Anya was fascinated to see how often her rabbit stopped to scrabble the snow away to nibble grass beneath, and she was amazed by how often it had a pee, leaving telltale orange marks. On a walk to the woods her family saw how easy it was to distinguish between rabbit, fox and deer tracks, and noticed how the distances between tracks varied, giving clues about the speed of movement.

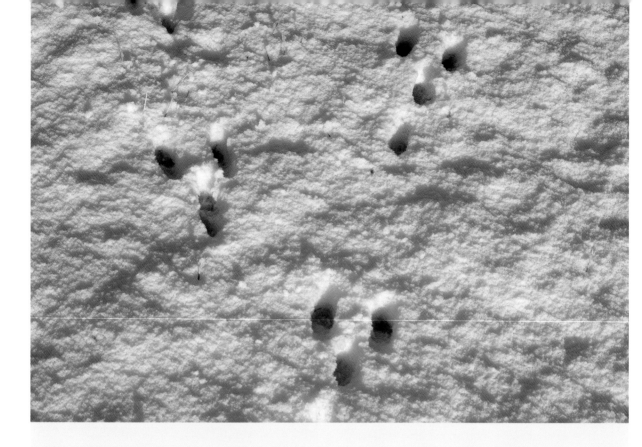

Tracking tips

- The best time to track is reasonably early in the morning.
- Tracks are most visible in soft mud, sand, or snow.
- Tracking is not a quick fix; it takes patience, perseverance and the ability to see subtle signs and clues. Find a place to sit and be still. Watch, listen and wait for the natural world to return to its undisturbed state. Then start to look around.
- Look in three dimensions (perhaps watching two-dimensional screens reduces our ability to peer right into the natural world). Try to pay attention to everything from the leaf right in front of your nose to the tree on the furthest horizon.
- Now start to move in search of clues. Look in the transition zones between habitat types, and try to get to know the habits of wildlife in the area.

Clues to look for

- **Tracks** Animals choose the paths of least resistance. Search for tracks on dirt roads or trails, perhaps leading to water or potential food sources.
- **Scat** Look for telltale animal droppings.
- **Ground spoor** – clues left on the ground: perhaps the remains of a meal, a den or areas of flattened vegetation where animals may have been lying down.
- **Aerial spoor** – clues above the ground, such as trees and shrubs that have been nibbled or rubbed against, or such subtle clues as broken spider's webs or ripped leaves.
- **Animal tracking guidebooks** Get a good book to help you identify tracks and other signs specific to your area (see page 157).

A TRACK TRAP

This is a simple way to find out which animals visit your back garden or use a path in the local woods.

Making a garden track trap

● Rake over an area of soil, and then smooth it by scraping a length of wood along it. Alternatively roll some clay out on an old tray or a flat piece of wood.

● Place some wild nuts, seeds or pet food in the middle of the prepared surface.

● Leave it overnight and return in the morning. Have there been any visitors?

Making a path track trap

● If you find a trail used by animals, pour water on a stretch of bare earth and make the surface as smooth as possible so that any new tracks will be clearly visible. Alternatively spread some clay along a section of path.

● Return the next day to check for telltale prints. To identify the animal, note the stride length as well as the shape of the prints.

TRACKING STICKS

The professional tracker is never without a stick to help train the eye and focus attention. These youngsters enjoyed scraping the bark off green hazel poles before carving one end to a point to make their very own tracking sticks.

Making a tracking stick

● Select a straight green pole and cut it to a length you are comfortable with, probably about belly-button height. The stick should be sturdy but not too thick or heavy.

● Scrape off the bark, using a sharp bushcraft knife, holding the stick at one end and moving the knife away from your holding hand and body.

● Carve one end to a point. To harden the point, hold it over a small fire for about five minutes, turning it constantly so that heat is applied evenly.

● Scratch lines on the stick at measured intervals and roll some tight-fitting elastic bands or O-rings along the stick.

● Complete the stick by carving the top into the head of an animal or bird; or, if you want to be really professional, glue a small button compass in the top (available from Internet suppliers at low cost).

● Use the lines and bands on the stick to record stride length and measure footprints.

Safety tips

● **Always supervise children when they are using bushcraft knives – see the tool safety tips on page 156.**

● **Be aware of fire safety tips – see page 156.**

BECOMING A STALKER

Tracking allows you to follow an animal at a distance, but stalking allows you to get up close. It's about moving softly and silently with every muscle under control, and being able to freeze instantly if the creature you are following shows the slightest sign of alarm. Becoming invisible isn't about disappearing; it's about becoming so inconspicuous that you almost become part of your surroundings.

What you need

● Shoes or boots with a soft sole to reduce noise; or better still, get in touch with the ground and go barefoot.

● Non-rustly clothing in natural colours, a close-fitting hat and soft gloves

● Face paint or mud to disguise the shape of your face

How to stalk

Animals are constantly alert for anything out of the ordinary, always looking out for something to eat or for something that might eat them. So as not to alert them, you need to move sympathetically with nature.

● Walk silently and slowly, ready to freeze instantly if need be. Keep your knees slightly bent and loose.

● Keep looking ahead, and with each and every step raise your foot and then place it down carefully, feeling the ground before committing your full weight. Move your foot to another spot if you feel a twig that might snap.

● Use a tracking stick (see page 115) like a third foot to help with balance, but always place it on firm ground.

● Choose your route carefully: read the landscape, look for cover, seek out places to hide.

● Use your senses of touch, sight, smell and hearing.

● Read the weather, particularly the wind direction. Always stay downwind of your target, with the wind blowing into your face.

● Keep on your feet until you get quite close to an animal. Then you may need to crawl or even lie down and squirm along on your stomach.

● Watch the animal you are stalking. Move only when it has its head down while feeding; if its head is up, stay as still as you can.

● When you are still, be calm, relax and breathe deeply; slide into the background. Perhaps you will be able to watch the natural world go about its business almost as if you weren't there.

TRACKING AND STALKING GAMES

You can introduce children and teenagers to tracking and stalking through games that encourage listening, looking and learning how to move silently. Try a silent version of capture the flag (see page 40), splitting into two teams and trying to get the flag by stealth rather than force. Or at a night-time outdoor gathering, get some members of the party to creep up on everyone else as they sit round the fire. We are grateful to Chris Holland, Martin Burkinshaw and Lynnie Donkin for sharing some of the following games with us at the 2008 and 2009 Wilderness Gatherings.

Safety tips

- **Have a central meeting place that everyone can return to.**
- **When following tracks and trails, insist that each child has a buddy and that they stay together at all times.**
- **Use only natural or biodegradable materials. Never mark trails with spray paint or other materials that do not decompose quickly.**
- **When taking part in blindfold games, move slowly and steadily; it's when children try to rush that accidents might occur. For children not used to this sort of activity, play in a large open space until they become accustomed to being blindfolded.**

TRACKING TRAILS

At Connie's tenth birthday party there was a rumour about treasure, so the girls were eager to try tracking. A prepared trail led them through the woods and they searched high and low for arrows and other clues, looking for anything out of place. Try setting up trails using natural materials as clues and signs at different levels. Although such games tend to be fast and furious, they are a good starting point before moving on to tracking for real. Making the clues harder to find slows down the pace.

How to play

An adult can set up the trail for all the children to follow, or split the children into two groups and get one group to lay the trail and the other to follow. Can the trail layers reach their destination before the followers catch up with them? Suggestions for trails include:

- **Arrows to show direction** Made from twigs, stones or leaves, or drawn in chalk, mud, charcoal from the fire or perhaps flour. Make the arrows on the ground or hidden in a tree.
- **Colours** Try smudges or arrows of natural colour in strange places, such as chalk on a tree trunk, blackberry juice smeared on a log, mud spread over a leaf or brightly coloured autumn leaves pinned to a tree trunk with thorns.
- **Materials out of place** Put acorns, fir cones, pebbles or other natural materials where they don't belong, and see if the trackers notice them.
- **Smell** How about using an onion to make a scent trail? Leave the trail on obvious landmarks such as gates, stiles, rocks or trees right next to the path. Use in conjunction with arrows to show direction.

FOX AND HOUNDS LOG DRAG HUNT

We saw a large group of children of all ages enjoying this game. Woods are a good place in which to play it, and it works especially well in the snow.

What you need
● A branch light enough for a child to drag along behind them, yet heavy enough to leave a trail. A twiggy branch works best, as it will leave a clearer trail in the earth and leaf litter. Alternatively ride a hobby animal (see page 97) to leave the trail.
● A short length of rope, which might make it easier to drag the branch

How to play
● One person is the fox and everyone else is a hound.
● Send the fox ahead to run through the woods, dragging the branch to leave a trail. The fox then chooses a place to hide.
● The hounds set off in pursuit, trying to follow the trail.
● Let everyone have a go at being the fox.

Variations
● Give the fox a bag of flour with a small corner cut off for leaving a flour trail.
● For a more challenging trail, use a lighter log to leave a less distinct mark, or use a pointed stick pushed into mud.
● Carve an animal footprint out of wood for the fox to press into the ground at regular intervals.

SNEAKY SNAKE GAME

This game is most fun if played in an area with trees, bushes and varied terrain. Ask everyone to stand in a line, holding the waist of the person in front. Give everyone a blindfold, except the person at the front, who leads the snake of children on an adventure, winding through trees, up banks and down hollows. If you have a very young group, they may prefer to play with their eyes open. Encourage everyone to be quiet – pretty impossible, as there's usually lots of giggling.

Try the following variations:
- Go barefoot and blindfolded.
- Play after dark but without blindfolds, giving the leader a red light to show the way without destroying night vision.

WOOD HIDE AND SEEK

When our children were small we often revisited a favourite woodland trail. A child and an adult would run ahead along the route and hide close to the path. The seekers would follow on behind and try to spot the hiders without leaving the path.

SLEEPING SQUIRRELS

This is a great way for children to experience natural sounds. Begin by talking about what animals might live in the area where you are playing. Then get everyone to lie on the ground and pretend to be one of those animals in a deep sleep. If you spot anyone moving, squirt him or her with water as a warning that they are out of the game! You can also play this at night with a torch.

SNEAKING GAME

We followed Chris Holland as he crept through the trees, moving smoothly and quietly. In contrast the children were a noisy rabble, excited to be heading into the woods; I wondered whether they would ever settle down to play a silent game. But once Chris got them sitting in a circle and the game began, they became completely caught up in the fun of stalking and sneaking as quietly as possible. The game is most challenging if the ground underfoot is slightly crunchy, such as a woodland floor with crispy leaves and dry twigs.

What you need

- A large Super Soaker water pistol or a plastic drinks bottle with a hole pierced in the lid, and a supply of water
- Noisy objects: perhaps a tin cup full of pebbles, a tambourine or a rustly crisp packet
- Blindfolds

How to play

● Ask everyone to sit in a circle and then place the noisy objects in the centre.

● Choose a volunteer to stand in the centre. Arm them with the Super Soaker and blindfold them.

● Another volunteer sneaks into the middle of the circle, moving slowly and placing each foot carefully on the ground, avoiding anything that might snap. The sneak tries to steal the noisy items from the centre and then return to their place, all without being detected by the person in the middle.

● If the person in the middle hears a movement, they try to spray the sneak. Any sneaks sprayed with water are out of the game. Random spraying of water is definitely not allowed!

● Everyone around the outside of the circle remains as quiet as possible.

● Give everyone a turn at sneaking and being in the middle.

Variations

● Tie little bells around the children's wrists or ankles, so that they have to creep really slowly to avoid making a noise.

● Put the noisy objects in a box or under a jumper, or tie them to a stick pushed into the ground so that the sneaks can't just run in, grab them and then dash out again.

● Do a version of bat and moth, where the blindfolded person in the middle of the circle calls out and the sneak has to echo a reply.

STALKING EACH OTHER

Practise your stalking skills while a friend pretends to be an animal. The game works best in a clearly defined wooded area. Perhaps the children could wear a headdress or mask of a favourite animal (see page 86), or ride off on a hobby creature (see page 97).

- While the stalkers count to 100, the 'animal' hides in the woods, somewhere he or she can keep an eye on all that is going on.
- The stalkers move slowly to look for the animal. If the animal spots a stalker he calls out and that stalker must identify him or herself.
- After about ten minutes the animal bangs a drum, hits two sticks together or calls out. Any remaining unspotted stalkers declare themselves. The winner is the person who got closest to the animal without being seen.

FOX AND RABBIT

Imagine a fox hunting at night, crouching and listening intently for his prey moving in the darkness. Predator and prey are relying on their finely tuned senses of smell and hearing; even the slightest rustle might give the game away.

How to play

- Play in an open grassy space; it's difficult to move quietly in woodland.
- Everyone stands in a circle, about an arm's length apart.
- One player is chosen as fox and another as rabbit. Both are blindfolded and spun around a couple of times. The fox then tries to track down the rabbit while the rabbit tries to avoid the fox.
- Neither the fox nor the rabbit should be allowed to stray beyond the circle.
- Everyone must keep quiet so that the fox and the rabbit can hear each other's movements. Can the fox track the rabbit down? Allow everyone to have a go if they wish to.

STALKING THE DRUM BEAT

What you need
- Blindfolds
- A drum or two sticks
- A water pistol or a plastic drinks bottle

How to play

- An adult or an older child sneaks off to hide in the woods with the drum or sticks and the water pistol. Once they are comfortable they put on a blindfold.
- Everyone else gets into pairs. One member of each pair is blindfolded; the other guides them into the woods.
- Allow a short time for the blindfolded children to get tuned in to the sounds and the feel of the woods. Children are always tempted to rush about, but a great way to help them slow down and get in touch with nature is to encourage everyone to go barefoot.
- The person who is hiding bangs the drum or hits the sticks together, giving a clue to their whereabouts. The blindfolded children try to follow the sound, showing their sighted partners where they wish to go.
- Meanwhile the drummer squirts the water pistol towards any sound of stalkers. Anyone who is squirted is out of the game. The pair who get closest to the drummer are the winners.
- Swap the pairs round and repeat the game.

TREASURE TRAILS

A treasure trail is a great way for children and teenagers to have fun outdoors using maps, following directions and finding clues, as well as encouraging them to work together. The real treasure is not what you find in the box at the end of the trail but the experience of finding new and special wild places along the way.

WILD TREASURE TRAILS

Fourteen girls were invited to camp in the garden for Connie's twelfth birthday. As many of them hadn't met before, we planned a wild treasure trail as an icebreaker. They glanced at the maps we gave them before running off to find the first clue, hidden in a plastic box. In their eagerness they ignored the map, relying on written clues and a trail of stick arrows we had left just in case. As they got further along the trail they became more and more engrossed, rising to the challenge of finding all six boxes.

What you need

- **Treasure boxes** Use small easily hidden weatherproof boxes.
- **Treasure** Connie's party treasure included bangles, hair ties, felt pens, plenty of sweets.
- **Maps and written directions** Place the directions in each box, giving instructions and directions to the next treasure box. Older children may be capable of relying on a map, but make sure it is accurate and detailed, and supply them with a compass.

Suggestions for clues

- **Simple bearings** For example, when two buildings, structures or landscape features are seen in alignment from a path. Our girls had to spot a windmill on a hill and then watch the slope beside them as they walked along; the treasure box was hidden beside the path near the point where the distant windmill disappeared behind the slope.
- **Camouflage trail** We laid a trail of brown wool from a waymarker post across the woodland floor to a hidden treasure box, leaving the end of the wool loose beside the box. We covered the wool trail with a thin layer of leaf litter to make it harder to follow. The girls were told to find the post and then follow the trail, but were warned not to pull the wool, or else they would lose the trail and never find the treasure!

- **Treasure in the canopy** We tied a treasure box on to the end of a long length of string, and Jake threw the box over a high branch. We left the box hanging high in the canopy, wound the rest of the string through the trees to make a trail and tied the end round a branch. The only way to get the treasure was to undo the string and follow the trail before lowering the box to the ground.
- **Hunt the flag** Edward scrambled into a tree to tie a small white flag on to the end of a branch, marking where the treasure was hidden in leaf litter below.
- **Photographic clues** The final box was hidden in ivy in the garden. The challenge was to locate the treasure from a photograph showing its location.

LETTERBOXING

Letterboxing is a navigational game that originated in Dartmoor in southwest England during the nineteenth century. It has become increasingly popular and has spread to many different areas. Participants use map reading and navigational skills to find hidden boxes; they may also need to solve complex riddles or find compass points. The boxes contain a visitors' book and a rubber stamp: letterboxers use these to mark their own record book, and also carry a stamp in order to leave their own mark in the visitors' book. The location of the letterboxes is often publicized through websites. Some boxes are easily accessible but others may involve an expedition into wilder country.

Try making up your own version of letterboxing to play in the local woods or Country Park. All you need is a few weatherproof boxes, some notebooks and stamps along with a good local map and perhaps a compass. This is an ideal activity for a family or for younger teenagers who want a little independence, and an excellent way to find out about map reading.

DIY LETTERBOXING

- Make up several boxes, each containing a rubber stamp, an inkpad and a notebook.
- Go out with a good map and hide the boxes. Record the grid reference for each box or just mark them on the map.
- Make up a letterbox trail sheet with each grid reference marked in order, or provide a copy of the marked map. Add a few additional clues and photographs to help find the boxes.
- Send a group of children off to follow the trail, collect all the stamps in their own record book and leave their own stamps in the boxes. Or several groups could compete to see who can collect all the stamps in the shortest time.

WOOL AND TAPE TREASURE TRAILS

A friend was throwing out an old videotape and wondered if he could use it for anything before getting rid of it. He came up with the idea of using the tape to make a trail. This would be ideal for younger children to follow, leading them all over the woods and in and out of the trees, winding in the tape as they go. Alternatively make an obstacle course by creating a beautiful spider's web of coloured wools in and around the trees, crisscrossing the strands. Each child follows one colour up and down ditches, over and under fallen logs, through muddy puddles and wherever it takes them, winding in the wool as they go until they reach the treasure at the end.

Safety tips

- Rushing off in search of treasure is exciting, a great chance to experience a sense of adventure and independence. However, it is vital that adults are always near by, making sure no one gets lost.
- Establish a base in a central open area and make sure an adult stays there at all times.
- Lay trails in an area that at least some of the children are familiar with.
- Make sure children stay together in groups or in pairs.
- Encourage children to keep in contact with adults via mobile phones or walkie-talkies.
- Always take home any non-natural materials.

TECHNO TRAILS

We once met a young woman who, despite claiming to have no interest in the outdoors, told us about a wonderful adventure she had had which involved scrambling over rocks and then crawling through a remote cave and putting her hand into a dark crevice to retrieve a treasure box. She had been led there with the help of a GPS device and returned home to log her find on the Internet. This is a perfect example of how modern technology can engage wider audiences with the wild world. If your children can't be persuaded to leave their gadgets at home, how about letting them run wild with them?

WALKIE-TALKIE TRAIL

How about using walkie-talkies outdoors to track down your friends at the park or in the woods? In this game two teams compete against each other.

● Half the members of each team (the hiders) go to find a secret base .

● Once the hiders have arrived, they talk to the rest of their team on walkie-talkies, directing them to the base. They can either use their own observations and notes of the route or give their teammates directions from a map.

● Each team must use a different channel. The winning team is the one that gets its team members to the secret spot first.

● The secret spot needs to be quite large so that the competing hiders don't overhear each other's instructions!

PHOTOGRAPH TRAILS

When we organized a photographic trail at an outdoor family event, we weren't at all sure how popular it would be. But everyone loved looking for the weird clay sculptures, the faces hidden in the trees and the elf fortress, all shown on a sheet of photographs. There were prizes for those children who made it to the den at the end of the trail and had their picture taken as evidence!

● Provide children with a sheet of printed photographic clues, or take the photos with a mobile phone and send them to the children's phones. Find the locations of all the photographs; perhaps the participants could take snapshots of themselves along the trail as proof that they found all the clues!

● Ask the children to photograph themselves doing things along a route: perhaps sitting on a particular stile, perching in a tree, balancing on a rock.

● Ask them to photograph natural materials instead of collecting them: for example, how many different flowers can they find on a route?

● Suggest that they take a cuddly toy or teddy bear for an adventure and photograph it at various points along the trail.

TEXT MESSAGE TRAIL

Lay a wild treasure trail as described on page 127, and text the clues to mobile phones. After discovering a treasure box, the children could perhaps solve a riddle and text the answer to the trail organizer, who then texts them the next clue. Make sure that you can get a phone signal at the site you are using!

GEOCACHING

This global treasure hunt combines using the newest technology with getting outdoors. Visit www.geocaching.com and you will see that hundreds of thousands of treasure boxes are hidden all over the world; we discovered several within a couple of miles of our home.

The game involves using a hand-held Global Positioning System (GPS) tracking device (available from outdoor suppliers), a GPS-enabled mobile phone or a mobile phone with a downloaded geocache navigator application to find caches. Information about the cache, such as coordinates, is posted on the website. A cache is usually a weatherproof box containing a logbook and a pencil along with small non-perishable treasure for swapping, such as toys, games or playing cards.

Once a cache has been found, the player may take a piece of treasure, provided they replace it with another item. Finds are logged on the website, and some players also post photographs taken at the cache. You can also hide caches yourself and post details on the website.

Having found the coordinates of a local cache on www.geocaching.com, we entered the numbers on a GPS device and set off in search of the treasure. The children were amazed to see that the device could show exactly where we were going and where we had been. Sadly we never found the cache, but the website had warned it was a particularly tricky one to find. GPS coordinates may only get you to within a few metres of a cache, so a useful tip for hiders is to post additional written clues on the website.

SETTING UP YOUR OWN LOCAL GEOCACHING TRAIL

One summer Kate Castleden, education officer at the Harcourt Arboretum in Oxfordshire, set up a local geocaching trail in partnership with the Institute of Physics. Families were provided with a GPS device and a leaflet that included a map, the GPS coordinates and written clues, which led them along a trail to find several caches. At each cache there was an activity to do, such as measuring the height of a tree. A friend's nine-year-old son and two reluctant teenage daughters were completely engrossed.

It's possible to set up your own trail like this, if you have a GPS-enabled mobile phone or buy a geocache navigator application for your mobile phone (see www.geocaching.com). Plan a route and hide the caches at points along the way, entering the coordinates of each cache into your GPS device. You could also make a paper guide with additional clues or riddles, or add to the challenge by asking the children to do an activity at each cache, such as taking a photograph, making an elf castle or designing a story picture. Split the children into teams; the first team to visit all the caches and carry out the activities is the winner.

Geocaching tips

● A GPS device is not a replacement for a map and a compass. Use it in conjunction with more conventional methods of navigating, including lots of common sense.

● GPS devices are best used when you are about 500m/500yds from your target, and should get you to within about 5m/5yds of it.

● Practise using a GPS device in your local area before using it to find treasure. Such a device works only when you are on the move and in areas open to the sky.

● Leave no trace (see page 156). When large numbers of people participate in geocaching, it can disturb wildlife and damage landscapes; search carefully for the boxes or caches and keep disturbance to a minimum. When hiding a cache, don't dig a hole or damage plants, and ensure it isn't visible to passers-by or in an environment that could be damaged by frequent visitors.

● If making your own trail for use by family and friends, clean the treasure up behind you. If intending to leave a cache in place for some time, ensure the box needs minimal maintenance.

● Always seal the cache and place it back exactly where you found it; don't be tempted to think you can find a better spot.

● Do not hide caches on private land unless you have permission to do so.

● For further details, see www.geocaching.com.

WILD ACTION

WILD ACTION

'I love waking up in the morning on the days I come here,' the fifteen-year-old boy said as he gently placed the roots of a young tree in the hole he had dug. 'I just can't wait to get started.' This was a boy who wasn't happy in school, a boy you wouldn't immediately expect to be absorbed by the natural world, but he was totally at ease and told us he hoped to work outdoors in the future. He was taking part in a Countryside Stewardship course at the Northmoor Trust's Little Wittenham Nature Reserve in Oxfordshire. This chance to get involved with practical conservation work had transformed his life.

Some teenagers may think voluntary conservation work is uncool, and it's unlikely to appeal to them at first; but we have found that once out there they tend to get really stuck in and enjoy using tools, learning a new skill, getting mucky and having some fun. Wild action like this is a chance to discover more about the natural world, enjoy a new challenge, accept responsibility, and just enjoy some exercise and fresh air.

This chapter is about taking time to look and discover more about what is going on around you. And it's about helping to conserve habitats, growing things, surveying wildlife – doing practical things that are not only rewarding and hugely enjoyable but also make a real and lasting difference.

WILD WATCHING

Every child on the beach suddenly stood still and gazed out to sea, transfixed by the sight of a huge osprey fishing just offshore. Despite beating its massive wings as hard as it could, the bird couldn't drag itself into the air because of the strength and determination of the large fish wriggling in its talons. A life-and-death struggle was unfolding in front of the children's eyes. Then, just as we all thought the bird was winning the battle, the fish tore itself free and fell back beneath the waves.

The children soon went back to their games, but for just a few moments they had been mesmerized, caught up in the dramatic intensity of the wild world.

We have shared some marvellous wildlife encounters with our children, including watching hundreds of bats pouring from a roof at dusk and spying on fallow deer in the woods behind our house. There are so many natural wonders to discover, from the flocking of tens of thousands of starlings at dusk to a baby frog's first leap from the garden pond or a snail emerging from its shell. It doesn't matter if you don't know what plants and animals live where or what anything is called; what matters is taking time to look and be amazed.

Fieldcraft

Discovering and enjoying nature's wonders takes a degree of patience, and the ability to look, take notice and keep an open mind: you never know what you will find. You will also need to become skilled in fieldcraft, the art of looking into the natural world, a chance to watch wildlife behaving naturally, as if we weren't there.

Fieldcraft tips

● If you buy one thing and one thing only it should be a reasonable pair of binoculars or a monocular. Once you are accustomed to using them they will allow you to enter a whole new world of wonder.

● Get up early and/or stay out late – this is when wildlife likes to be about.

● Camouflage yourself, try to blend in to natural shapes around you and keep below the skyline. Follow the tracking and stalking tips on pages 112 and 116; be slow and patient and avoid sudden movement.

● You may be sitting still for a long time, so wear several layers of clothes and take gloves, hats, a warm drink and something waterproof to sit on.

● Use photography to record what you see. If photographing an insect or a wildflower, it can be useful to put a coin beside them to give an idea of scale.

Join a survey

One May evening we joined an organized badger watch in some local woods. We were sent off in small groups to various locations and for two hours we sat silently, watching, waiting, listening. This was a chance to get up close to wildlife and contribute to research about badger populations. Taking part in an organized survey is a way to share discoveries and contribute to our understanding of biodiversity, through finding plants and animals and recording them with a note, a sketch or a photograph, or looking for the clues they leave behind.

A shelter hide

The best way to get up close and personal to wildlife is to make a hide. Use natural materials to make a small shelter or den where you can become invisible. This could be anything from a branch held over your body to a sturdy natural shelter. Try making a simple hide by pushing a bendy branch into the ground and then bending it over to make an arch. Bend a second branch over at right angles to the first, and then cover the arches loosely in branches or netting. When making a hide, follow the BLISS formula:

- **B for blend** – a hide must blend with its surroundings.
- **L for low** – a hide's silhouette should not intrude on the view or break the skyline.
- **I for irregular** – follow nature's example and avoid straight lines.
- **S for small** – the less the impact on the environment, the less the chance of being spotted.
- **S for secluded** – choose an out-of-the-way place off a busy path.

The no-hide hide

It's all up to you! Wear natural-coloured clothes, blur the shape of your face by painting it with mud or natural face paint (see page 89) and use natural objects such as branches to hide your shape.

A camouflage blanket

Hide beneath a blanket and disappear from view. Camouflage fabric is available to buy, but try making your own by weaving leaves and grasses through garden netting.

DISCOVERING WHAT'S UNDER YOUR FEET

Our children used to spend hours rummaging in the soil of our allotment, searching for treasure such as the remains of old clay pipes, weathered glass and colourful pottery fragments. A friend's son took this a stage further and made his own little museum in a garden shed. Anya tried to find out more about the treasures she collected on local walks, inventing all sorts of wonderful stories about them. There was a little brown glass bottle that had contained a witch's poisonous potion; a hip flask dropped by a Victorian farmer; another bottle dropped by a cowboy in the 1760s; and a steel spoon used by a soldier. She labelled each find and offered visitors a guided tour of her collection.

Outdoors beneath our feet there is soil, rock, water and all the creatures and microbes living within the soil, but there are also intriguing clues about the lives of those who went before us. Most everyday things of the past have disappeared, but some durable items survive under the ground for years, making tantalizing clues for archaeologists to piece together to create a picture of how people lived.

BURIED TREASURE

We went off to the woods with a group of four-year-olds armed with trowels in search of tiles and pottery near the site of an old kiln. Each child enjoyed digging up fragments of tile, and back at school they made their own little tile houses for imaginary elves. Try having a mini-archaeological dig in the back garden or the corner of the school field. The trick is to work slowly, scraping away a bit of soil at a time and investigating every little thing you come across.

What you need
● Old clothes to wear – be prepared to get muddy
● Spade and tools for scraping and searching, such as a garden trowel, a paint scraper or a plastering trowel
● Plastic containers – one with water in for washing your finds and others for sorting
● Old sieves, paint brushes, labels and permanent markers
● A box in which to display your finds

Becoming a garden archaeologist
● Choose where to dig your trench. Try to find a place where there might be a good chance of finding something, such as at the end of a garden, where there might have been a bonfire or a building in the past, or on an old allotment. Never dig holes in the ground on other people's land without permission. Try not to dig in the middle of an immaculate lawn!
● If digging in a grassy area, start by removing turves; keep them ready to be replaced when you have finished. Make the trench a regular shape so that you can be methodical. Split the trench into sections so that everyone gets a turn. Try to record finds as you collect them.
● If you find something sticking out of the ground, don't try to pull it up; instead, scrape the soil away little by little until you can gently lift the object from its resting place.
● Keep an open mind and encourage children to treat each and every find as special, whether it's a rusty bit of metal, an animal bone, a fragment of weathered glass or china, or an old clay pipe. Don't forget to keep an eye out for interesting creepy-crawlies as well.
● Once you have completed your dig, carefully return all the soil and replace any turves.
● Encourage the children to display their finds in little boxes, labelling each discovery

DOWSING

My cynical teenagers were very dubious about this activity. How could
a stick possibly move of its own accord? But as my father and his friend
Malcolm walked along, each holding a forked twig, the twigs suddenly
gave a sharp tug and bent down towards the ground. It wasn't until
Hannah and Edward had a go with their grandfather that they realized
this was no hoax; they too felt the unstoppable force of the twig turning
in their hand, indicating the presence of water below the ground.
This was water divining, otherwise known as dowsing, a powerful
and mysterious phenomenon.

Dowsing involves using simple hand-held tools to search for hidden things. It is used across the world to search for underground features such as water, cavities, metal and lost items. Dowsers have the ability to use a natural sensitivity; perhaps they pick up clues subliminally from the environment, which enables them to find things we simply cannot know about. The tool is just a mechanism: whether or not dowsing works for you is a function not of the tool but of your subconscious and your openness to the process. Children often have a natural flair for dowsing, perhaps because they are less sceptical than adults. So have a go and be amazed!

What you need

Various tools can be used for dowsing. Find a method that works for you.

● **A forked stick** Cut a forked flexible twig of hazel or willow, making sure that the two arms of the fork are similar in size and shape. Trim the ends, and then grasp an arm in each hand, palms uppermost and thumbs facing out from your body in opposite directions. Hold your elbows tightly against your waist and then spread the fork slightly apart, with the main stem pointing directly away from you and parallel to the ground.

● **Rods** A pair of L-shaped rods made out of fencing wire or a metal coat hanger. The shorter arm of each rod should be slightly longer than the width of your hand and the longer arm about 25cm/10in. Hold the shorter arm of the L in a closed palm with the longer sections facing forward and parallel to the ground. Your hand should only be touching the shorter arm, so that the longer arm can turn freely.

● **Pendulum** We had a go with a pendulum made with a cork, needle and thread. You could make a pendulum – perhaps from a favourite stone or crystal or perhaps a fir cone or shell.

How to dowse

● In order to avoid disappointment, have a go first with someone who has dowsed before, so that you can get a feel for it and see how it works.

● Choose an outdoor area in which to dowse – perhaps the back garden, a wild space or the school playing field.

● Select your method and hold the instrument as appropriate.

● Walk slowly and steadily over the patch of ground you have chosen, focusing on what you are doing, perhaps asking yourself questions in your head. Clear your mind of everyday thoughts and focus on your dowsing tool, feeling for movement. If your dowsing is successful, the twig will bend towards the ground, the wires will turn in your hand or the pendulum will swing.

Dowsing activities

● Have a go blindfolded across an area where you know there is water, such as an old well or underground drain.

● Hide a coin or a box of treats in an area. Can anyone find it by dowsing?

● Try dowsing for water in an open space, and each time your dowsing tool indicates there is water put a stick on the ground. If you do this several times, in an area does a pattern emerge?

GROWING YOUR OWN FOOD

Going to the allotment always seemed to be a bit of an adventure for our children: they played with the soil, hunted for creepy-crawlies and sowed seeds and loved to graze on freshly harvested carrots, beans and raspberries. Growing food provides a real insight into natural cycles as well as the pleasure of growing and eating your own food and enjoying spending time outdoors together.

Don't be too ambitious: you could start with herbs in pots on a windowsill, cherry tomatoes in a hanging basket or lettuces in plastic storage boxes outside a classroom, on a terrace or balcony. Some plants grow pretty quickly; the spicy leaf mizuna, for instance, can be sewn in autumn and will be ready for harvesting on Christmas Day. If you have access to a garden, let the children have a corner to call their own or give them their own tub of soil; perhaps they

could even start up their own little enterprise. My cousin's daughter Connie was given a little plot of land in the garden and told that any money she made from it would be hers. She rose to the challenge, taking over a disused shed as her potting shed and creating a miniature market garden. She looked after her plot meticulously and set up a little stall from which to sell her home-grown produce to passers-by.

MAKING A DIFFERENCE

The group of teenagers tumbled out of the minibus, laughing and joking as they ambled slowly towards the wood. Their teacher provided them with an assortment of tools and they set to work straight away, building a boardwalk across the muddy ground. They clearly enjoyed being outdoors and working together, and knew that their project would allow more people to visit a special place. If given the opportunity, many children and young people rise to the challenge of practical conservation projects, enjoying an enormous sense of escape and fulfilment.

Most of Europe's landscape is a mix of managed habitats at different stages of succession; practical work includes clearing scrub to benefit grassland, planting trees and coppicing woodlands. In places where true wilderness remains there is less need for habitat management, and practical work might be related to visitor access, such as path improvements and making boardwalks and hides. Conservation

work can also involve making gardens better places for wildlife, by providing bird boxes and feeders, bumblebee houses and bat boxes, and creating new habitats by, for instance, digging ponds and planting trees.

We have found that children and teenagers enjoy many of these activities, as we hope the following pages will show.

TREE PLANTING

As part of my parents' golden wedding celebrations, my father asked each of his three daughters and seven grandchildren to plant a tree at Dun Coillich, a community-owned nature reserve in Highland Perthshire in Scotland. We gathered together on a chilly October morning to plant trees in celebration of fifty years past and as a link to the future of a special place. Whenever we return to Perthshire, the children make sure we check that their trees are growing healthy and strong.

Across the UK community woodlands are becoming increasingly popular, planted to provide a habitat for wildlife, a local amenity and a future source of firewood and other wood products. When planting trees always consider how large they may grow and make sure you choose species to suit the size of the site. Try to choose native species for maximum benefit to wildlife.

Growing trees from seed

Following an autumn walk we got home to find the children's pockets heavy with acorns. We shoved them into pots full of soil and promptly forgot all about them. The following spring we discovered several vigorous young oak trees, apparently thriving on neglect.

If you wish to grow trees from seed, go for a local walk and collect seeds and nuts when they fall to the ground in the autumn. Collect from naturally occurring trees, as these will be of most benefit to your local wildlife. Put the seeds in pots of soil or compost and leave them outside. Place netting over each pot to prevent mice and other creatures from eating the seed, but remove the netting after germination. Leave the young tree in the pot for a couple of years before planting it in a suitable environment where there is enough space for it to grow to its full size.

How to plant a small tree or shrub

- Always plant trees and shrubs in the winter or early spring.
- Wiggle a spade backwards and forwards in the ground to make a wedge-shaped slit, about the depth of the spade. Make sure the hole is large enough for the roots.
- Take your shrub or tree and gently twist the roots so that they are wound together in a bunch; this makes it easier to put them into the hole.
- Place the shrub or tree in the hole with every bit of root below ground level. Make sure the plant is vertical and use your foot to push the soil down firmly all around the stem.
- If using a cane to support the young plant, push it into the ground close to the stem. Twist a rabbit guard around the plant and the cane. Remove these once the plant is established.
- Planting the shrub or tree is not the end of the story. In a dry summer it may need watering, and in a warm wet summer you may need to pull out vigorous weeds so that it's not smothered.

LIVING WILLOW STRUCTURES

Our friend Nigel worked with our local primary school to make a wildlife-friendly, adventure-inspiring, living play space out of a few stems of willow. Living willow domes, tunnels and mazes are great projects for families and groups; willow is wonderful to work with and pretty much refuses to die, although it will need yearly maintenance.

What you need

- Long straight rods of bendy willow. Avoid crack willow or weeping willow, but any other variety is suitable. Try using fresh cut willow from your garden, or from a local farmer or park manager who has been cutting willow trees back. Alternatively purchase from a specialist willow supplier (see page 157), who will probably supply willow-weaving instructions as well. Always use the willow rods within a week of being cut.
- Secateurs
- Metal stake for making holes in the ground
- Manure or compost
- Long strips of inner tube or natural cordage (e.g. honeysuckle or ivy stems) to tie the willow rods in position

Making a willow dome

● Make your willow dome during the winter or early spring.

● Choose a site: willow structures grow more or less anywhere but prefer moist soil and an open site with plenty of light. The roots are pretty invasive, so don't plant willow over drains or underground pipes or near buildings or walls.

● Decide how large you want your shelter to be; this will depend on the length of the willow and how much space you have. The willow should be long enough to bend right over so that it almost touches the ground on the other side of the dome, as illustrated. Mark a circle on the ground and decide where the entrance will be.

● If the soil is poor, dig a trench around the circle and line it with manure or compost to ensure your willow gets off to a good start.

● Push the willow rods into the ground at even intervals around the circle, leaving a gap for the entrance. To provide stability and increase the chance of successful rooting, push each rod down to about 22–30cm/9–12in. The whole job is easier if the ground is soft, so try to choose a day just after it has rained. If the ground is very hard, water it first and you may need to use a metal stake to make holes.

● Match a willow rod with another one on the opposite side of the circle, and then bend them over towards each other. Tie them together with long strips of inner tube or natural cordage. Carry on doing this all the way around the circle until you have created a dome. Interweaving

the rods at the top will increase stability.

● Now take some smaller willow rods. Push one in beside each of the larger rods, and then bend them over at an angle around the outside of the dome to make a lattice effect. Tie them in position. Keep doing this until you have worked all the way round. This dome has two smaller willow lengths beside each upright, to make a denser lattice. Try to make yours symmetrical.

● Using these principles, you can make tunnels, mazes, thrones or whatever structures you like!

Looking after willow structures

A healthy and vigorous willow structure requires some maintenance:

● Water the plants occasionally, especially if the first summer is very dry.

● Weed around the base of the plants if need be, or cover the ground around the dome with a mulch of woodchips or leaf litter to suppress weeds.

● Weave new growth back into the structure to fill in gaps and add strength.

● Willow grows very quickly and you will need to cut it back each year.

BASHA BOATS

For groups not too sure about taking part in conservation projects, try combining practical work with a fun activity. How about using the brushwood produced from coppicing, pollarding or clearing scrub to make a basha boat? You will need a pond or lake to sail your boat across!

At a Wilderness Gathering we joined instructor Joe O'Leary and his team from Wilderness Survival Skills to make a simple basha boat with a large group of excited children. We were impressed by the simple design, the speed with which a watertight floating craft was made and the fact that it actually worked. Children as young as four were involved with every step of the process and then had fun racing the boats on the lake. This would be a great activity for a party or gathering on a warm summer's day – water fights are inevitable!

You will need

● 16 stakes (2.5cm/1in diameter hazel is perfect) with sharpened tips, 8 of them about 120cm/4ft long and the rest about 60cm/2ft
● A waterproof tarpaulin
● Large amounts of brushwood and bendy green twigs – hazel is perfect
● Plenty of strong string
● Life jackets and paddles

Making a basha boat

● Lay the tarpaulin on the ground to get a rough idea of the final size of the boat. We used a very large tarpaulin, so we folded it into four. You could use a smaller tarpaulin, provided you make the brush ring small enough for the tarp to wrap right around its edges (see below) and it is thick enough not to be punctured by the brushwood.

● Remove the tarpaulin and stick about ten of your stakes in the ground in an oval shape within its area. Make another inner ring by placing the rest of the stakes inside the oval.

● Place the brushwood in between the inner and outer stakes to make a doughnut-shaped ring, pushing it down as you work. A young child might find it fun to stamp carefully around the top of the ring to compress the brushwood.

● To sew the ring together, sit a child in the middle of the doughnut shape. Tie a ball of string to the end of a chunky stick (your needle) and then, using your foot, lift the twigs slightly so that you can feed the needle underneath the brush to the child in the middle, who can then pass it back over the top to you. Bind the doughnut all the way round, removing the stakes as you go. It is very important to pull hard and tight to keep the tension on each turn.

● Push the longer stakes through the middle of the brush to make a lattice for the base (as illustrated), hammering the ends to get the stakes through both sides if necessary.

● Cover the prepared tarp with bracken or grass to protect it from being pierced by twigs.

● Place the doughnut on top of the tarp; there should be just enough tarp to wrap around the sides. Tie the corners of tarp down with strong string to the deck stakes, keeping tension, and then continue tying all the way round until it is secure.

● Ask for brave volunteers to check out the floatability and watertightness of your craft!

Safety tips

● **Supervise children very carefully when near water and when handling sharp tools and sticks.**
● **Make sure no one goes in a basha boat without a life jacket on.**
● **If in a river or anywhere with a current, tether the boats to the land.**

153

MORE ABOUT
RUNNING WILD

MORE ABOUT RUNNING WILD

**For more information about outdoor activities and our other books,
Nature's Playground, *Go Wild!* and *Make it Wild!*, please visit
www.goingwild.net.**

LEAVING NO TRACE

All the activities in this book should be carried out with the utmost respect for the integrity of the natural world. Run Wild with minimal impact by respecting all wildlife, being considerate to other people, disposing of waste properly and taking responsibility for your own actions. Only collect loose and plant materials that are common and grow in abundance, and leave wild places as you found them.

WORKING WITH GROUPS IN WILD PLACES

When taking groups of children to wild places, consider the following:
● Make sure you have the landowner's permission to use a site.
● Always have consideration for other users of the countryside and for wildlife.
● Ensure there are plenty of adults to help with supervision.
● Establish some kind of central meeting point and make sure everyone knows what to do if they get lost.
● Have some simple ground rules and make them clear from the start.
● Only you know how responsible or competent the children in your group are, so give freedom accordingly.
● Always carry a basic first-aid kit.

FIRE SAFETY

When using fire, always follow these basic safety tips:
● Make fire on mineral soil (not on leaf litter or vegetation), in a pit or a fire pan.
● Don't light a fire in windy or excessively dry weather conditions, as it could get out of control.
● Never leave a fire unattended.
● Have a supply of water near by in case you need to extinguish the fire or soothe burns.
● Use as little wood as you can and let the fire burn down to ash. Once it is cold, remove all traces of your fire.
● Always supervise children and young people when they are using fire.

TOOL SAFETY

Tool safety is about knowing how to use tools responsibly and appropriately as well as being aware of, and avoiding potential dangers.
● Always have a first-aid kit handy and ensure someone present knows how to use it.
● Make sure everyone is aware of the potential dangers of using sharp tools. Accidents usually happen when people are messing around.
● Before using a knife, make sure there is an imaginary 'no entry' zone all around you. Stand up with your arms spread out and turn around; you shouldn't be able to touch anyone or anything.

● Think about follow-through. Where is your blade likely to go if it slips? Is there anything or anyone in the way?

● Never cut over your lap. The femoral artery in the thigh carries large volumes of blood and if it is severed you could lose a pint of blood a minute.

● Work the blade away from your body, and away from the hand supporting the wood. Never cut towards your hand until you can use a knife with great control.

● Always cut on to a firm surface such as a steady log.

● If you need to pass a knife to someone else, always do so with the handle pointing towards the other person.

● Always put knives and axes away in their sheaths when not in use; never leave them lying around.

● At the end of each activity session we always collect knives and other tools and put them in a bag together. Young people need to realize that knives should be used only when participating in craft and conservation activities; a knife is a tool and never a weapon.

● Give knives and other sharp tools the respect they deserve: always stick to the rules.

CHAPTER REFERENCES

Wild Games

The World Beach Project, www.vam.ac.uk

Wild Stories and Wild Theatre

Holland, Chris, *I Love My World*, Wholeland, 2009;
www.wildwise.co.uk and
www.wholeland.org.uk
MacLellan, Gordon, *Celebrating Nature*, Capall Bann Publishing, 2007
www.creepingtoad.org.uk
Hastings, Jeremy, www.islaybirding.co.uk
Mask ideas: www.maskmaker.com

Wild Trails

Maxwell, Ian, *Animal Tracks ID and Techniques*, Flame Lily Press, 2007;
www.shadowhawk.co.uk
For information about geocaching:
www.geocaching.com

Wild Action

Suppliers of willow withies:
www.willowwithies.co.uk and
www.windrushwillow.com
Willow weaving: www.wyldwoodwillow.co.uk
Wilderness survival skills:
www.wilderness-survival.co.uk

USEFUL ORGANIZATIONS

Organizations that offer conservation activities in the UK

The British Trust for Conservation Volunteers:
www.btcv.org
The National Trust: www.nationaltrust.org.uk
County Wildlife Trusts: www.wildlifetrusts.org
The John Muir Trust: www.johnmuiraward.org
The Duke of Edinburgh's Award: www.dofe.org

Other useful organizations and websites

www.aonb.org.uk
www.bgci.org
www.breathingplaces.org
www.forestry.gov.uk
www.naturalengland.org.uk
www.playengland.org.uk
www.woodlandtrust.org.uk
www.wildernessgathering.co.uk
(the UK's annual bushcraft festival)

INDEX

ACKNOWLEDGEMENTS

Thanks to everyone who has shared ideas and provided practical advice and support. If there are inadvertent omissions in these acknowledgements, please notify the publisher, who will rectify them in future editions.

We would like to thank the following people for their help and advice: Jane and Bob White; Jeremy Hastings (Islay Birding), Chris Holland and Chris Salisbury (Wildwise), Jon-Paul Lamoureux, Martin Burkinshaw, Lynnie Donkin, Joe O'Leary and everyone else who shared ideas with us at the 2008 and 2009 Wilderness Gatherings; David Gosling; David Millin; Jenny Crook; Gordon MacLellan (working as Creeping Toad); Robin Hull; Malcolm Appleby; James and Helen Jackson; Heather Frances; Nigel Adams; Kate Cheng; Iain Naismith; Ollie Rathmill; Chris Parker; Kate Castleden at the Harcourt Arboretum and Alexandra Cheung at the Institute of Physics for information about geocaching trails; Polly Scott and her reception class; Caroline, Colin, Clifford, Frankie and Anya Carr; and the many other families and friends who have supported us in so many ways.

A big thank-you to all the young people who took part in activities: Tom U; Jonathon and Jessie A; Lily, Charlie and Toby R; Agnes K; Carolyn S; Clifford, Frankie and Anya C; Anna, Tim, Nicholas and Ella V; Alice F; Fiona and Eliza N; Tilly S; Lucas R; Rebecca and Edward W; Harry G; Alexander B; Matt, Tris and Will E; Rory A, Tom P, Sean W, James D, Natasha and Adam H; Anna, Laura and Ben W; Sophie T; Isabella G; Catherine F; Milly B; Tilly G; Rebecca M; Lydia, Helena and Lucian S, David C; Milly H; Christopher and Sienna W; Scott H; Ama and Mahalia J; Danny, Jess and Natali K; Kate W; Tsering L; Ella W; Jess R; Imogen B, Hannah M, Sarah P, Ellen B, Rose P; Kerry W; Libby and George W; Hamish, Isobel and Oliver M; Magnus G; Josh G; Tiggy W; Milissa D, Harry F, Yanni K, Arthur K, Harry T, Jack M, Olly P, Sam B, Anatol S, Gabriel G, Daisy and Olly C, Tallula, Noah and Poppy C, Georgia E, Connie B, Scarlet R, Carla, Louie, Stan and Frankie C, Holly P.

Many thanks to our husbands, Ben and Peter, and our children, Jake, Dan, Connie, Hannah and Edward, for all their support.

And finally, thanks to everyone at Frances Lincoln who has helped *Run Wild*, our fourth book, become a reality.